Praise for

The Small Group Lea

"You can't get more practical than Dave Earley. This book will help small group leaders determine the tools they need to develop for a successful ministry. This more than a book. It is an implementation guide. Get your pen out and see where this takes you."

SCOTT BOREN

Pastor and author of "The Relational Way"

"This book hits the key points of leadership and prescribes remedies for one of the major problems facing congregations in today's church. Dave Earley provides a realistic method for developing leaders. Our church has grown into one of the largest in America and development of leaders is an ongoing challenge that must be addressed if we are to continue to reach new believers for Christ; Dr. Earley confronts this problem and offers practical solutions. This book should be required reading for leaders in any growing church."

DEAN RUSH

Pastor of Ministry Operations, Community Bible Church, San Antonio

"When I read Dave's best-seller, *8 Habits of Effective Small Group Leaders,* I knew I was holding the definitive book on small group leadership. Now I have two contenders competing for that title. The content and personal worksheets for this book are transformational!"

RANDALL NEIGHBOUR

President, TOUCH Outreach Ministries and author of "The Naked Truth About Small Group Ministry"

"It doesn't get any better than this! Put aside any other book you are reading and pick this up. Dr. Earley has written a readable, practical, applicable and motivational book on leadership development that will change your life, the lives of those under and around you as well as the very life of the church. Dave has taken 30 years of experience in the local church developing leaders and put it in a form everyone can understand and use. It is spiritual leadership for the 21st century."

DAVE WATSON

Lead Pastor, Calvary Chapel, New York City

"Dave Earley's ministry and resources have become a vital part of the development for each Lifegroup leader in our church. This book is very practical and highlights the essential elements of an effective small group leader and ministry. I am excited about the way Dave simplifies the ten power tools for personal leadership development."

SCOTT SHIELDS

Lifegroup Pastor, North Asheville Baptist, Asheville, North Carolina

Praise for

The Small Group Leader's Toolkit

"Dave Earley knows what he's talking about when it comes to small groups. Through years of putting these principles into practice in a local church context, he has a lot to offer those committed to genuine biblical community through small groups."

TRENT KIRKLAND
Lead Pastor, Zion Church, Clarion, Pennsylvania

"I work with leaders every day. This book is just the ticket! It's insightful, zeroing in on key disciplines that effective small group leaders possess. It's also practical, giving simple steps to help leaders develop those disciplines. I plan to use several chapters when I pull my small group leaders together for training. I'll put copies of this book in my small group leader's hands as well. Every small group leader should study this book until he or she masters all ten of these tools."

JAY FIREBAUGH
Director of Small Groups, New Life Church, Gahanna, Ohio

"I have worked with Dave for 20 years and he knows small groups from the inside out. He understands the importance of small groups and how they can help grow and develop disciples. This book should be a part of every small group leader's library . . . and every pastor should read it carefully to make better disciples!"

DR. ROD DEMPSEY
Discipleship Pastor, Thomas Road Baptist Church
Chairman, Department of Discipleship Ministries, Liberty Theological Seminary

"Small groups are central to the New Testament paradigm for growing strong disciples. Dave Earley has given us an excellent resource to help pastors and church leaders with the nuts and bolts of how to go forth and build small groups into the life and ministry of the local church. The relevance of materials like this for fulfilling the Great Commission cannot be overstated."

DR. RON HAWKINS
University Vice Provost for Distance Learning and Graduate Studies
& Professor of Counseling, Liberty University

"Because leadership is often misunderstood or feared, many have fallen short of their potential to serve God and the church. Rooted in abundant research and experience, Dave Earley has provided an excellent tool which gives clarity and understanding to the biblical principles and practices of leadership. Though the intent is for small group leaders, this book is beneficial for leaders in *all* levels of church leadership!"

STEVE COFFEY
President, Christar

THE SMALL GROUP LEADER'S
TOOLKIT
TEN POWER TOOLS FOR PERSONAL LEADERSHIP DEVELOPMENT

THE SMALL GROUP LEADER'S
TOOLKIT

TEN POWER TOOLS FOR PERSONAL LEADERSHIP DEVELOPMENT

DAVE EARLEY

TOUCH® Publications
a division of TOUCH® Outreach Ministries
Houston, Texas, U.S.A.

Published by TOUCH® Publications
P.O. Box 7847
Houston, Texas, 77240, U.S.A.
800-735-5865

Cover design by Mark Neubauer Design
Editing by Randall G. Neighbour

ISBN 978-09788779-7-2

TOUCH® Publications is a book publishing division of TOUCH®
Outreach Ministries, a resource and consulting organization for
churches with a vision for a cell group or holistic small group-based
local church structure.

To order additional copies of this book and other resources written
by Dave Earley, visit http://www.touchusa.org

Connect with the author at: http://www.daveearley.net

ACKNOWLEDGMENTS

There are many people I need to thank for shaping my life as a leader and a leader of leaders.

Thanks to Lee Simmons, and Roy Rhoades who asked me to lead my first small group when I was sixteen years old.

Thanks to Doug Randlett who asked me to lead a small group and coach a basketball team when I was 19.

Thanks to Dane Emerick who encouraged me to lead a dorm full of young men.

Thanks to Eddie Dobson who allowed me to lead 300 campus small groups.

Thanks to Rod, Steve, Chris, and Brian who followed my leadership to plant a church.

Thanks to Cathy who has been following my leadership for 27 years.

Thanks to Daniel, Andrew and Luke who are supposed to have been following my lead as long as they have been alive.

Thanks to all the people who have been in groups I have led through the years.

Thanks to Larry Gilbert who let me train leaders in national seminars.

Thanks to John Maxwell who encouraged me to steal his best ideas.

Thank to my pals at the Center for Ministry Training who follow my leadership now.

Thanks to my students at Liberty University and Liberty Theological Seminary who challenge me to live what I teach.

Special thanks to Randall and Etna Neighbour whose contagious passion to equip small group leaders is changing the world.

YOUR TOOLKIT

INTRODUCTION:
The Determining Factor

"Everything rises and falls on leadership" - Lee Roberson[1]

Several years ago I was dissatisfied with my church, my small group, my marriage, and my children. So, being the spiritual giant I am, I asked God to change *them*.

God's response was swift and clear. He said and did absolutely nothing.

So I again asked the Lord to change them. Again, He said and did nothing.

Then I asked a third time for the Lord to change them. This time, His response was unmistakable: "The one who needs to change is *you*."

He was right. I had little or no control over others. The only one I really had the power to change was myself. So, I invested two years studying everything I could find related to leadership and worked hard to become a better leader.

Everything does rise and fall on one's leadership ability. As I became a better leader, my small group grew and multiplied. My church multiplied leaders and set attendance records. My marriage improved. My children also stepped up to reach their potential.

In this book, I want to give you the basic leadership principles and tools needed to become a better small group leader. You can also apply them to any other ministry in which you are involved or your business or family. These leadership principles are simple, practical, and powerful tools that will help you become a better leader in any relationship or setting.

Before you dive into this toolkit of leadership, I want to discuss seven reasons why developing your leadership skills is vitally important.

Leadership ability is the determining factor. The single greatest hinderance to ministry growth is the lack of true leadership.

The greatest strength a ministry possesses is not money, space, evangelism, or resources. It is leadership. The greatest problem a ministry faces is not money, space, evangelism, absenteeism, or resources either. It's leadership! All other factors being equal, leadership ability will determine the *size* of your ministry, the *quality* of people in your ministry, the *number* of leaders within your ministry, the *morale* of your ministry, the potential *growth* of your ministry, and the long term *impact* of your ministry.

Leadership ability determines the size of a person's ministry.

When I read Jesus' parables, I find God gives more to those who have shown the ability to be trusted with more. Our wise and benevolent God will not increase or expand a person's ministry if he or she is not doing a good job loving and serving the few He has already given.

Leadership ability determines the quality of people in a person's ministry.

I have a friend who is a quality leader. She works hard and her ministry has doubled in the last two months. The number of leaders serving under her has grown from none to four.

Despite her success, she is frustrated with the man who serves as the head of her ministry. Every time we visit, she shares comments like, "Dave, I just don't understand. Why can't he see this?" "Why doesn't he do that?" and "I don't want his job, but I can't understand why he won't do it!" She is wrestling with the decision quality leaders always face when they serve under less developed leaders: "Do I just focus on my ministry and let the rest of this ministry suffer, do I talk to his superior, or do I find another ministry?"

If her boss does not step up and do a better job of leading, he will lose her. Quality leaders are attracted by serving those more developed than themselves, but *repelled* by serving leaders of a lower caliber.

Leadership ability determines the number of leaders in a person's ministry.

Leaders who consistently multiply their groups attract and develop new leaders constantly. If you struggle to find anyone to train so you can multiply your small group, it could be you have not attracted any leaders to your group.

Leadership ability determines the morale of a person's ministry.

I currently serve at a seminary that struggled to attract students. A few years ago, we appointed a new leader with the tools and temperament needed to thrive in our setting. The morale of the faculty and staff shifted dramatically. Then, student enrollment numbers took off.

When a leader with abilities is at the helm, morale remains high and it makes all the difference in the world.

Leadership ability determines the long term impact of one's ministry.

Let me give you an example from church history. George and John were contemporaries who both had great results preaching the gospel. Their messages shook two continents for Christ.

Everyone agreed that one was the better preacher, yet he was not much of a leader. The other was adequate in the pulpit, but was an exceptional leader.

Few people outside of a seminary have ever heard of the preacher named George Whitefield. However, John Wesley's ministry lives on through the ministry he established. Today there are 70 million Methodists who trace their roots back to Wesley's leadership![2]

Leadership ability allows a person's ministry to multiply

I will never forget a display I saw at the Museum of Science and Industry in Chicago years ago. It featured a checkerboard with 1 grain of wheat on the first, 2 on the second, 4 on the third, then 8, 16, 32, 64, 128, etc. Somewhere down the board, there were so many grains of wheat on the square that some were spilling over into neighboring squares . . . and there, the demonstration stopped. Above the checkerboard display was a question, "At this rate of doubling every square, how much grain would be on the checkerboards by the 64th square?"

To find the answer to the riddle, I pressed a button on a console and the answer flashed on a little screen above the board: "Enough to cover the entire subcontinent of India 50 feet deep."[3]

Never underestimate the power of multiplication.

The slow process of raising up multiplying leaders is the fastest way to fulfill the Great Commission. In fact, it is the only way. The world is growing by multiplication and the church is growing through addition. In order to catch up and keep pace with the multiplying population of the world, you must multiply *multipliers.*

In other words, it takes a leader to make a leader who makes other leaders. Before you can multiply leaders from your small group or your church, you must become a leader who strategically creates a legacy.

Leadership ability enhances a person's ability to handle changing and challenging times.

No generation in history has been forced to navigate the levels and speed of change found in the world today. Leaders who navigate change successfully enjoy an exciting ministry full of growth. In fact, there is no growth without change. If a ministry hopes to grow, it must be confidently prepared to change. All over North America, church leaders have discovered that the church must change or die. Yet many crash on the rocks of under-led change.

In order to lead your small group through change effectively, you must become a leader who employs the power tools described in this book. If you attempt to lead without them, needless fear and frustration, pain, and problems will arise.

GOD IS LOOKING FOR LEADERS

In His infinite wisdom, God has chosen to implement His ministry on earth through you and me. He does not have to use us, but that is the path He has selected.

This means that God is always on the lookout for leaders. His desire is to find them and get fully behind them, as He told King Asa:

> *For the eyes of the LORD range throughout the earth to strengthen those whose hearts are fully committed to him.*
> (2 Chronicles 16:9)

When people refuse to allow God to lead them, he removes His blessing. Read the blood-curdling words He gave King Saul:

> *But now your kingdom will not endure; the LORD has sought out a man after his own heart and appointed him leader of his people, because you have not kept the LORD's command.*
> (1 Samuel 13:14)

Read what God said to Ezekiel:

> *I looked for a man among them who would build up the wall and stand before me in the gap on behalf of the land so I would not have to destroy it, but I found none.*   (Ezek. 22: 30)

That verse is one of the saddest in the Bible. Because of a lack of leadership, a nation was destroyed. But it is also one of the most encouraging statements ever made. If there had been a leader, a nation would have survived. One leader *can* make a big difference. You have what it takes to be that leader!

Kingdom business is the *most important* business.

One of my friends is a pilot for United Airlines. Twice a year he receives two weeks of intense training. That's four weeks a year, or 160 hours of training. Why? Untrained pilots put hundreds of people at risk and will quickly become bad for business.

Let me ask you a question. If a pilot is required to receive extensive training to sharpen his skills because he holds physical lives, how much more should you receive training to develop your skills? When you lead a small group, you hold eternal souls in your hands! Kingdom business is the most important business on earth.

It is more difficult to lead unpaid volunteers than paid employees.

In many ways, church leadership is more difficult than secular leadership. One cannot motivate a volunteer with a pay raise or the threat of a pay cut. Church leaders not only need to be as good as secular leaders; they need to be better! The ten power tools described in the following pages will help you lead, love, motivate, train, and release others. With hard work and dedication, you will help unpaid volunteers become passionate ministry leaders.

Leadership can be learned and developed.

A man was once asked if any great leaders were born in his hometown. He replied, "No, just babies."

Leaders are made, not born. While it is true that a few people possess the natural abilities, intelligence, background, or training to be a 10 out of 10 on a leadership scale, everyone has room for improvement. You may not jump from 2 to a 10 by simply reading this book. But you could go from a 2 to a 5 or from a 5 to 7, which will make a huge difference in your ministry. As a spiritual leader, every step up the scale you make increases your impact for God exponentially. Employ what you find in this book and watch your ministry as a small group leader flourish with growth!

Chapter One
PRAYER

It was late August and I was facilitating our annual training for leaders and their apprentices. We used this time each year to prime our leaders for another season of effective small group ministry. To kick off the event, the small group coaches introduced each of the leaders they supported. Then, the leaders introduced their apprentices to everyone.

Bob, who led a men's small group, stood up and introduced Rick as his new apprentice. I thought to myself, "Bob, you are wasting your time."

Bob and his coach were reliable leaders and I trusted their judgment. However, in this situation I was sure they were making a mistake. Rick was a great guy with a sweet-spirited wife and son. He was faithful and had a super attitude. But he was an ordinary guy. I was convinced Rick did not possess the leadership abilities to grow and multiply a small group.

One year later, we began our annual training day with the introduction of new leaders. I have to admit that I was very surprised when Rick was introduced. I was also stunned when he introduced a new Christian named Mike as his apprentice. Mike, much like Rick, was a quiet, behind the scenes "ordinary guy."

When Rick sat down, I thought to myself, "Sure, Rick is a new leader, but the new group must have launched because Bob did such a good job growing it. Bob must have been desperate and needed someone to take over a new group. Rick will never be able to grow it and multiply it."

The next year, we began our day of training the same way. I was floored that Rick was not only still leading a small group, but that Rick's former apprentice, Mike, was introduced as a new leader! Rick had not only grown his group, but he multiplied it.

This was no fluke. Year after year, Rick grew and multiplied his group. Before long, he was coaching several men's groups and continued to lead a small group.

After that second year, I was curious to find Rick's secret of success. I asked Rick's coach about Rick. He observed, "Rick does everything we ask him to do like other leaders. But what sets him apart from others is that he prays a lot. Every night in fact. Rick prays with his wife too. Every day while he works, he prays for his group and his men. The guy has an incredible prayer life, and it shows."

The next time I saw Rick, I asked about his prayer life. He was almost embarrassed to tell me how much he prayed. "I know I can't do ministry without God," he said. "So I put my energy into asking Him to do it through me."

After thirty years of leading groups and training leaders, I am convinced that Rick has hit the nail on the head. If a leader only has one tool in their leadership toolkit, the tool they need is prayer. It is not the only tool, but it is the single tool that makes every other tool effective.

Prayer is the secret

Several years ago I had the opportunity to hear a man teach whom many considered the greatest authority on spiritual leadership. It was one of the last public talks ever given by former Oriental Missionary Society Director J. Oswald Sanders. I will never forget what he said:

> Leadership is influence . . . Since leadership is the ability to move and influence people, the spiritual leader will be alert to discover the most effective way of doing this . . . Prayer influences men by influencing God to influence them.[1]

Read that last sentence again. Leadership is influence. One of the most powerful ways to influence others is through prayer. Therefore, to lead effectively by influencing others for God, Christian leaders must have prayer in their toolkit.

I have studied the lives of God's greatest spiritual leaders from Abraham to Billy Graham. It is my conclusion and conviction that prayer is the timeless—and often overlooked—secret to high impact spiritual leadership. Certainly courage, faith, giftedness, and abilities help make leaders spiritually influential. I agree that godly integrity, ardent passion, clear purpose, and solid plans are important. It is important to cast vision, identify core values, and mentor a team of leaders. But the foundational skill and common denominator of great spiritual leaders and dynamic spiritual influencers down through the ages is rooted in prayer. Prayer is the ageless act of highly effective Christian leaders.[2]

Hudson Taylor was an English missionary to China. He founded the China Inland Mission that became miraculously influential for God in China. At his death, the mission included 205 mission stations with over 800 missionaries and 125,000 Chinese Christians. How did he do it? He discovered, "It is possible to move men through God by prayer alone."[3]

PRAYER IS THE MOST IMPORTANT TASK OF A SPIRITUAL LEADER

There are many important tasks for the effective small group leader. Great leaders invite, contact, prepare, and plan. But Christian leadership is spiritual work. Spiritual work depends upon spiritual tools. No spiritual tool is as significant or powerful as prayer. As Andrew Murray reminds us, "In spiritual work everything depends upon prayer."[4]

Murray's words are not merely speculation. They are substantiated by research. For example, a survey of small group leaders revealed an interesting correlation between time spent in prayer and small group multiplication. It revealed that leaders who spent 90 minutes or more in daily devotions multiplied their groups twice as often as those who spent less than half an hour with God.[5]

Prayer is powerful

Through the years I have found that I was not alone in my belief that prayer is the missing ingredient. This truth is echoed from one end of the theological scale to the other. On one end of the theological continuum we have John Wesley who wrote, "God will do nothing on earth, except in answer to believing prayer." On the other end we have John Calvin, who states, "Words fail to explain how necessary prayer is . . . while God never slumbers or sleeps He is inactive, as if forgetting us, when He sees us idle and mute."[6]

Billy Graham has observed, "Today the world is being carried on a rushing torrent of history. There is but one power available to redeem the course of events, and that is the power of prayer . . ."[7]

Pray or quit!

Then Jesus told his disciples a parable to show them that they should always pray and not give up (Luke 18:1).

Pray or quit. That's the choice Jesus knew His disciples would face. He knew that the relentless rigors of high-octane ministry would induce burn out if they did not develop a strong connection to the Father. The pace would be too demanding, the opposition too brutal, people problems too frequent, and the need too overwhelming. They needed to fully employ the tool of prayer or they would throw their hands up and quit.

Small group leadership is tough and unrelenting as well. It can be one of the hardest, yet most fulfilling challenges you can accept. So often it demands immense patience and perseverance. It is extremely hard to continue working and waiting for a harvest that seems slow in coming. At times it feels like the enemy is fighting you every step of the way. You need strength and encouragement in strong doses. Grace and strength to help in time of need is found at the throne of God and is accessed by prayer.

Prayer saves time

Charles Spurgeon was an incredibly successful and busy English pastor. He led England's first multi-mega church, trained leaders, started a college, and wrote extensively. He also understood the profound priority of prayer. When preaching on the subject of prayer he observed,

> Sometimes we think we are too busy to pray. That also is a great mistake, for praying is a saving of time . . . God can multiply our ability to make use of time. If we give the Lord his due, we shall have enough for all necessary purposes. In this matter seek first the kingdom of God and his righteousness, and all these things shall be added to you. Your other engagements will run smoothly if you do not forget your engagement with God.[8]

The leaders of the largest small group-based churches in the world take time to pray. One South Korean pastor whose church has thousands of small groups stresses the importance of prayer:

> One of the greatest lies of Satan is that we don't have enough time to pray. However, all of us have enough time to sleep, eat, and breathe. As soon as we realize that prayer is as important as sleeping, eating, and breathing, we will be amazed at how much time we have to pray.[11]

INTERCEDE FOR THOSE YOU SERVE

Effective spiritual leaders are passionate toward God and compassionate toward people. Through prayer, God will give you a burden or a holy concern for those you are called to lead. You may not always accept their behavior and poor choices, but you will develop an unconditional love for them.

One of the purest and most powerful ways for a leader to express and exercise such love is in intercessory prayer. "Love on its knees" is the definition and description Dick Eastman gives to intercessory prayer.[12] Such prayer seeks the best for others before the throne of God and brings their needs to the One who has the answer.

A study of the lives of high impact spiritual leaders reveals that they made a time investment to pray for their people. Consider Moses. His primary ministry as he led the Hebrews through the wilderness can be summarized in six simple words: *"So Moses prayed for the people"* (Numbers 21:7). Moses was an unusually effective spiritual leader because he cared enough for his people to pray for them.

The term *intercede* means "to go between." It describes the act of going to God and pleading on behalf of another.[13] Generally speaking, "prayer" is defined as conversing with God concerning anything and anyone, including one's self. Therefore, all intercession is prayer, but not all prayer is intercession.[14]

Intercession was a major part of the leadership ministry of Moses. Again and again in the books of Exodus and Numbers, we read about Moses effectively crying out to God on behalf of his followers (Exodus 17:4; Numbers 11:2; 14:13-19).

Many Christian leaders pray too little in general and even less for others. If this describes your prayer life, this must change. Intercessory prayer is the primary tool used by effective spiritual leaders.

Missionary leader Wesley Duewel writes, "You have no greater ministry or no leadership more influential than intercession."[15] It was E.M. Bounds who said, "Talking to men for God is a great thing. But talking to God for men is greater still."[16] S.D. Gordon said, "True prayer never stops in petition for one's self. It reaches out for others. Intercession is the climax of prayer."[17]

The great leader and prophet Samuel felt it to be sinful to fail to pray for his people. He said to his people, *"As for me, far be it from me that I should sin against the LORD by failing to pray for you"* (1 Samuel 12:23).

The Apostle Paul was a major league difference maker. His letters are washed in his intercessory prayers for his followers:

God, whom I serve with my whole heart in preaching the gospel of his Son, is my witness how constantly I remember you in my prayers at all times. (Romans 1:9-10)

I have not stopped giving thanks for you, remembering you in my prayers. (Ephesians 1:16)

I thank my God every time I remember you. In all my prayers for all of you, I always pray with joy. (Philippians 1:3-4)

We always thank God, the Father of our Lord Jesus Christ, when we pray for you... For this reason, since the day we heard about you, we have not stopped praying for you... (Colossians 1:3,9)

We always thank God for all of you, mentioning you in our prayers. We continually remember before our God and Father your work produced by faith, your labor prompted by love, and your endurance inspired by hope in our Lord Jesus Christ. (1 Thessalonians 1:2-3)

With this in mind, we constantly pray for you...
                                    (2 Thessalonians 1:11)

I thank God, whom I serve, as my forefathers did, with a clear conscience, as night and day I constantly remember you in my prayers.   (2 Timothy 1:3)

Jesus *lived* intercession. His entire story is identifying with us, standing in our stead, and going to God the Father on our behalf. As a leader, He prayed for His followers. In speaking of His twelve He said, *"I pray for them"* (John 17:9). In speaking of His then future followers—you and me—He said, *"I pray also for those who will believe in me through their message"* (John 17:20). Even now in His exalted home in Heaven, Jesus is the One *"who is even at the right hand of God, who also makes intercession for us"* (Romans 8:34 NKJV) and *"who always lives to make intercession"* for us (Heb. 7:25 NKJV).

If you want to lead like Moses, Paul, or Jesus, you need to pray like Moses, Paul, and Jesus.

Effective leaders elevate their followers over themselves

Moses knew that one of the base-line attitudes of an effective leader was that one's followers come first. In a stunning announcement in Exodus 32, God offered to destroy Israel and start over, making Moses into a great nation. Wow! All of his whiney headaches would be gone and he could become the father of a nation . . . heady stuff for anyone to consider. Although it must have been a tempting offer, Moses did not give this a moment's thought. He immediately asked God to spare the people.

If that seems like a supreme act of selflessness, note that Moses takes it one step further. One of the most stunning, revealing, and challenging verses in the Bible on the subject of great leadership is found at the end of Exodus 32. Moses pleaded with God to spare the rebellious Hebrews under his care:

> *So Moses went back to the LORD and said, "Oh, what a great sin these people have committed! They have made themselves gods of gold. But now, please forgive their sin—but if not, then blot me out of the book you have written."*   (Exodus 32:31,32)

I am amazed at the sacrificial selflessness of Moses. He was willing to lose his own reservation in paradise if it would keep them from being destroyed. Moses was a great leader because he was a great servant.

Great leaders are willing to sacrifice for their followers. Consider the heart of the apostle Paul who cried, "I could wish that I myself were cursed and cut off from Christ for the sake of my brothers, those of my own race, the people of Israel" (Romans 9:3). Wesley Duewel adds:

> We must so identify with those we lead, both by love and by commitment, that we carry them on our hearts every day of our leadership . . . we must touch His throne constantly for our people. We sin against the Lord if we fail to do so.[18]

"Try tears"

Think of the spiritual leader Jesus, whose heart for hurting people was summed up in two words: *"Jesus wept"* (John 11:35). Consider how He became a man of sorrows and acquainted with grief (Isaiah 53:3). See Him lament, *"O Jerusalem, Jerusalem . . . how often I have longed to gather your children together, as a hen gathers her chicks under her wings, but you were not willing!* (Luke 13:34). Notice the tears streaming down His cheeks when he contemplated the pain of the people:

> *When he looked out over the crowds, his heart broke. So confused and aimless they were, like sheep with no shepherd.*
> (Matthew 9:36, *The Message*)

> *As he approached Jerusalem and saw the city, he wept over it.*
> (Luke 19:41)

> *During the days of Jesus' life on earth, he offered up prayers and petitions with loud cries and tears to the one who could save him from death, and he was heard because of his reverent submission.*
> (Hebrews 5:7)

William Booth was an unconventional, controversial zealot for Jesus. He lived the life of a spiritual soldier as the founder of the Salvation Army and preached to the least of the least. Two of his protégés set out to find a new work, only to meet with failure and opposition. Frustrated and tired, they appealed to Booth to close the rescue mission and release them from their obligation. General Booth sent back a telegram with two words on it,

"TRY TEARS"

They followed his advice and they witnessed a mighty revival.[19]

Resilient triumphant intercession converts the lost

Persistent faith-based intercession produces results. No one symbolizes this better than George Müller. In 1884 he testified that forty years prior, five individuals were laid upon his heart. He interceded for them to come to Christ, yet eighteen months passed away before the first was converted. He prayed on for five additional years and another was converted. He continued to pray. At the end of twelve and a half years, the third was converted.

He said that he continued to pray for the other two, without missing a single day, but they were not yet converted. But he was encouraged that the answer would come.[13] In fact Müller said, "They are not converted yet, but they will be."[14]

At his death twelve years later, after interceding for them daily for a total of fifty-two years, they were not yet converted. But one came to Christ at Müller's funeral and the other shortly thereafter![15]

How to intercede effectively

Suggestions for better intercession:

1. Pray for others the way you wish others would pray for you.
2. Focus your prayers on the spiritual issues of eternal significance more than the material, physical, and temporal needs of others.
3. Use scriptural prayers when appropriate. Below are two prayers Paul prayed for his followers, which are excellent examples:

> *For this reason, since the day we heard about you, we have not stopped praying for you and asking God to fill you with the knowledge of his will through all spiritual wisdom and understanding. And we pray this in order that you may live a life worthy of the Lord and may please him in every way: bearing fruit in every good work, growing in the knowledge of God, being strengthened with all power according to his glorious might so that you may have great endurance and patience, and joyfully.*
> (Colossians 1:9-11)

> *And this is my prayer: that your love may abound more and more in knowledge and depth of insight, so that you may be able to discern what is best and may be pure and blameless until the day of Christ, filled with the fruit of righteousness that comes through Jesus Christ—to the glory and praise of God.*
> (Philippians 1:9-11)

Do it!

As I stated earlier, if you can only have one tool in your leadership toolkit, it should be prayer. Prayer gets God in on the act. Prayer makes everything better. Prayer expands time. Prayer is potentially very powerful . . . if you take the time to do it. It all boils down to making prayer your first priority.

I don't know how you would rate your prayer life on a scale of 1 to 10. Wherever you are, determine to take it to the next level. If you only pray a few days a week, pray every day. If you pray 15 minutes a day, pray a half-hour. If you pray a half-hour a day, go to a full hour. If you have one prayer time, try two. When you choose to become a person of prayer, you'll have the most powerful tool created for a spiritual leader.

Your Prayer List

List the names of your small group members:

_____

_____

_____

_____

_____

List the names of your family members:

_____

_____

_____

_____

List the names of unchurched friends and neighbors:

_____

_____

List the names of coworkers, fellow students, or others:

_____

_____

_____

After you complete this page, make a copy and put it in your Bible.

The Small Group Leader's Personal PRAYER Worksheet

This week I purpose to deepen and strengthen my prayer life by:

❏ Replacing _____ minutes of TV or Internet use with prayer.

❏ Beginning each day by talking and listening to God.

❏ Talking to God as I drive to work instead of listening to news or music.

❏ Asking God to speak to me as I fall asleep each night.

❏ Making a special appointment with God to pray *more* one day this week.

   That day will be: _____.

❏ Lengthening my daily prayer time to _____ minutes a day.

❏ Other:

I will share these goals with _____ so he or she can encourage me to follow through and hold me accountable.

My daily prayer time/times will be: _____ am/pm _____ am/pm.

The amount of time or times I will pray are : _____ minutes at a time,

_____ minutes a day.

My place for prayer is: _____

I have a place to journal my answers and requests: ❏ Yes   ❏ No

Chapter Two
PERSONAL INTEGRITY

When I was a young pastor, one of my heroes fell. He was the most gifted Bible teacher I had ever known. Brilliant and full of charisma, he was able to make overlooked sections of the Old Testament burst into life. As a speaker, he was in strong demand.

Yet, the last time I heard him speak, I sensed something was off. Uncharacteristically, he labored through his message as if the whole process was up to him. I did not sense the usual anointing that had always marked his delivery. What was wrong?

A few weeks later it all made sense. The truth came out that he had cheated on his wife.

His lack of integrity was devastating. It hurt his children, his wife, his health, and the many people who looked to him for leadership. Those closest to him wrestled with intense feelings of shock, anger, betrayal, and deep hurt. He had sinned, cheated, lied, denied, and deceived.

Of all people, he knew better. It never had to come to this. But it did. His church and family were left to wade through the aftermath of this awful, ugly episode.

As he shared with us years later, he was so busy that he neglected his personal time with God. Because of his great gifting, he thought he could live without personal accountability.

One of the most important tools any leader can keep in their leadership toolkit is personal integrity and character. It is also the most dangerous tool to leave out. Without integrity, a leader is living dangerously. Satan will surely exploit this vulnerability.

What is Christian Integrity?

Christian integrity is living life based on biblical principles and godly values. It is linked with responsibility, honesty, morality, loyalty, being trustworthy, and responding to temptation with incorruptibility. Integrity could be described as having the courage to always do the right thing because it is right, no matter what. It is achieved by accountability.

We often link the concept of integrity with Christian character. Through the years, I have been collecting definitions and descriptions of Christian character. Some of my favorites include:

Character is what a man is in the dark.

Character is who you are when no one is looking.

Character is measured by what you would do
if you were never found out.

Reputation is what men think you are.
Character is what God knows you to be.

Abraham Lincoln observed, "Character is like a tree and reputation like its shadow. The shadow is what we think of it; the tree is the real thing." A newspaper columnist noted, "The best index of person's character is how he treats people who can't do him any good, and how he treats people who can't fight back."

Andy Stanley said, "There is never a reason to compromise God's standards in order to maintain God's blessings." The United States Air Force Academy defines character as "the sum of those qualities of moral excellence that stimulates a person to do the right thing, which is manifested through right and proper actions despite internal or external pressures to the contrary."

You must have integrity!

If a small group leader lacks integrity two things will happen. One, they will not be able to effectively grow and lead a group because people will not trust them. Or if they lead people, the people will ultimately be crushed by the leader's lack of integrity. When it comes to your Christian integrity, you must not cut corners.

Building a Life of Biblical Integrity and Godly Character

You don't just wake up one morning and look in the mirror to see a man or woman of biblical integrity. Integrity and godly character are built up little by little, day after day, choice-by choice, incident by incident. Integrity is not automatic. It is consciously cultivated. It happens on purpose. Integrity is not a gift. It is the reward of discipline, sacrifice, honesty, consistency, and doing what is right regardless of the cost.

After hearing my friend's painful account of resigning from his church because of moral failure, I decided to write out the non-negotiable commitments required to build and maintain biblical integrity and godly character. Here's what I wrote to myself:

Your personal time with God is vital – prioritize it.

When I consistently spend time with God, I have the strength to say "no." It also helps me correct small cracks in my character before they become canyons. My friend struggled to consistently spend time with God. A lack of intimacy with God caused him to seek intimacy in all the wrong places, with the wrong people, at the wrong time, and in the wrong ways. Have you prioritized time with God, or does He get leftovers?

You have emotional, spiritual, and physical tanks – keep them "topped off."

Human beings are made up of body, soul, and spirit. Yet, we are more than three isolated compartments. The state of one area affects the others.

I know that I am more susceptible to temptation when I am physically tired, emotionally drained, or spiritual spent. As a leader, I am expected to fill other people's tanks. However, I cannot expect others to fill mine. I have learned how to best replenish my tanks to keep them full.

I carefully monitor how many hours of sleep I get each night. If I sleep less than seven hours too many nights in a row, my physical tank is empty. When I exercise regularly, I feel better physically and emotionally and I sleep better. These are practical ways I keep my physical tank full.

Keeping a journal helps me manage my emotional life, so I write in it each day. I also find that my emotional tank is drained by unresolved conflict or broken relationships, so I seek to resolve disputes quickly. Spending too much time with draining people can be hazardous to my emotional health as well. Trying to minister beyond my areas of giftedness also empties my tank. On the other hand, quality time with my family fills my emotional tank.

Do you know what drains your emotional, spiritual, and physical tanks and how to fill them?

You have a few priority relationships – build them.

Too often, leaders spend so much time ministering to others that they have nothing left for their families. One way I have overcome this is to do ministry with my family. When my boys were in high school, we led a multi-small group ministry for high school kids in our home. We may have been going in different directions all week, but on Wednesday nights we knew we were at home doing small group ministry together.

Other family pegs we kept nailed down were family dinner five nights a week around the kitchen table, family devotions a couple of nights a week, and prayer with each boy before bedtime. Family vacations and celebrating birthdays are also important elements in prioritizing relationships.

For Cathy and me, a favorite marriage building priority is our weekly date. It may be lunch and frozen yogurt, or a hike, or a bike ride. Three Fridays out of four, we know we will enjoy a good block of undisturbed time together.

In what ways are you prioritizing your most important relationships?

You must please only one person – choose the right person!

You cannot live a life of godly integrity when you live to please yourself. However, you will also get in trouble when you try to please others. Focusing on your image or appearance will cause you to stretch the truth and cover mistakes, ultimately stealing your integrity.

Do you strive to please yourself, others, or the Lord?

Your time on earth is a blip on the radar screen of eternity – stay focused.

Eternity has been compared to the efforts of a parakeet picking up a single grain of sand in its beak and flying to the moon to drop it off before returning home to repeat the process. If each trip took a million years, and the parakeet worked hard until every single grain of sand was on the moon, it would take billions and billions of years. And that would be just a *moment* in eternity.

Our lives here on Planet Earth are merely a blip on the radar screen of eternity. We must refuse to be distracted by temporal temptations and worldly priorities. We must use each day to prepare for an eternal tomorrow.

Think about your current dreams and priorities in life. What impact will these things have five hundred or a thousand years from now in eternity?

You are the product of your habits and personal disciplines – develop good ones.

The decisions you made yesterday determine who you are today. The choices and disciplines you make today will determine your tomorrows. Basic habits such as Bible reading, prayer, journaling, reading books to sharpen yourself and your ministry, investing time into other believers in worship, community and fellowship, tithing, and serving the community never go out of season.

Do you want to know what kind of person you'll be in the future? Look at the decisions you are making today.

You need accountability – seek it out.

The Bible is clear about our need for one another. When God declared that it was "not good that a man should be alone"; He proclaimed the essential relational side of our DNA. Just as we all have a genuine God-shaped void in our hearts, we also have a human-shaped one.

You were never intended to go it alone. In fact, isolation often leads to a downfall. You will never reach your potential without the help of others. You need accountability.

As I look back on my life, I have made an important discovery. I have enjoyed the greatest levels of personal growth and spiritual victory during the years when I intentionally maintained a regular accountability time with another man of God. Remaining utterly honest and open about my habits made all the difference in the world.

Because of this realization, I touch base with my accountability partner once a week without fail. Since we both travel to speak in churches most weekends, Monday is an especially good day for us. Often, we eat lunch together. Or, he pops into my office and asks how I am doing. I have requested that he hold me accountable by asking me the following questions every week:

• Have you consistently spent time with the Lord?
• Have you been morally pure in thought, word, and actions?
• Have you watched anything, read anything, looked at anything, or visited any web site you would be embarrassed to view with Jesus?
• Have you written, spoken to, or touched anyone inappropriately?
• Have you honored and invested in your wife?
• Have you lied about any of these questions?

The key to success with accountability is inviting someone you trust to hold you to an account in the weak areas of your character.

THREE TESTS EVERY LEADER FACES

The Test of Morals

We live in a culture that glamorizes and celebrates what you can get away with. Dishonesty, lying, cheating, and stealing is expected as long as you don't get caught. Sex before marriage is expected. Extra-marital affairs are common.

Pornography is a multi-billion dollar business. Statistics for Christians trapped in the grips of pornography are alarming.

In a 1995 survey by Patrick Means of 350 men (10% pastors, 90% key laymen from twelve denominations), 64% admitted to struggles with sexual addiction or sexual compulsion, such as use of pornography, compulsive masturbation, or other secret sexual activity; 25% of married men admitted to having committed adultery; and another 14% confessed to sexual contact short of intercourse.[1]

In a 1992 survey of 800 active church members and leaders, 15% of the men and 11% of the women admit to having been unfaithful to their spouses, and 49% had viewed pornography in the past year.[2]

91% of men raised in Christian homes were exposed to pornography while growing up (compared to 98% of those not raised in a Christian home).[3]

I feel their pain. I was exposed to pornography at the age of seven. Sadly, it left a deep scar on my heart and mind. Lust became an especially difficult challenge for me to overcome as a teenager. Yet, it had to be overcome if I hoped to fulfill my destiny as a Christian man, husband, father, and leader . . . and it has. Praise the Lord! My honesty, plus personal accountability, plus absolute dependency on God's all-sufficiency has led to my on-going victory.

Immorality is always very costly and spiritually deadly. No one can afford to pay its crushing price. Joseph had the integrity to not only refuse the temptations of Potiphar's wife, but to literally run out of the room when she threw herself at him repeatedly. If he needed to run, so must we!

I find I can easily avoid lust as long as I refuse to get near temptation. Below is a list I have developed that keeps me pure.

I will never...

• Gaze at a pornographic web site or download pornography.
• Visit an "adult" bookstore or look at a "men's magazine."
• Go to a "gentleman's club."
• Watch an "adult" video or movie.
• Engage in a personal phone call or email exchange with a female other than my wife without my wife's knowledge.
• Read a questionable novel or book.
• Look closely at a female below her chin.
• Be alone with a woman in any setting for any reason at any time unless she is old enough to be my mother or grandmother.

- Share my personal, emotional feelings with any female other than my wife.
- View another woman as anyone other than a person for whom Jesus suffered, bled, and died.

For the ladies, my wife suggests the following list to remain pure. I will never...

- Read a trashy romance novel.
- Engage in personal phone calls or email exchanges with a male other than my husband without my husband's knowledge.
- Look closely at a male below the belt.
- Be alone with a man in any setting for any reason at any time unless he is old enough to be my grandfather.
- Share my personal, emotional feelings with any male other than my husband.
- View another man as anyone other than a person for whom Jesus suffered, bled, and died.

The apostle Paul was clear: it is not enough to try to stop a negative habit. A positive habit must be put in its place. In other words, put off the old successfully by putting on the new. When it comes to the moral test, I have also developed a mental list that helps me.

Instead of wasting thought, time, money, and energy in that which is immoral, I will ...

- Wash my brain in the living waters of the Word of God each day.
- Memorize the Word regularly.
- Pray for my spouse daily. (If you are single, pray for your future mate daily.)
- Have a connecting conversation with God each day.
- Have a connecting conversation with my spouse each day.
- Remember that an earthly life of purity will enable me to better experience an eternity of ecstasy.

What habit or practice tests your morals? What moral things must you do to replace any immorality in your life?

The Test of Money

Bob and Janet loved leading their small group. Unfortunately, they also loved to spend money . . . money they did not have. One day, they realized they had accumulated over $20,000 in credit card debt apart from their mortgage and car loans. Swimming in debt, they teetered on the verge of bankruptcy.

Then Bob heard a Christian finance show on the radio. The host stated, "Bankruptcy is listed in the top 5 life-altering negative events that we can go through, along with divorce, severe illness, disability, and loss of a loved one. I would never say that bankruptcy is as bad as losing a loved one, but it is life-altering and leaves deep wounds both to the psyche and one's credit report."[4] This jarred Bob. After a conversation with Janet, they decided to get help.

They went to see a debt counselor and created a plan to get out of debt. Unfortunately, in order to stave off bankruptcy, Bob needed to work a second job delivering pizza at night. On top of her day job, Janet watched a toddler for a single mother who worked nights. This kept them out of bankruptcy, but also took them out of small group leadership.

Learn from Bob and Janet's mistakes! Money becomes a test to our integrity when we begin to love it more than serving God. Jesus strictly warned about the intoxicating power of money. Paul also had much to say about the negative aspects of loving money.

We live in a materially-obsessed culture. The media constantly bombards us with, "spend more and possess more!" Money—and the things it can buy—are presented as the key to happiness. Because of this, the number of Americans drowning in debt is staggering. Many small group leaders are unable to effectively do ministry due to an extraneous debt load. To dig their way out of unnecessary debt, they sacrifice time in ministry for overtime at work.

Fortunately, the Bible is a great guide for avoiding financial bondage. In fact, the book of Proverbs offers six simple steps to finding financial freedom.

1. Stay out of debt.

The rich rules over the poor, and the borrower is servant to the lender (Proverbs 22:7).

Debt can be distressing, demoralizing, divisive, and devastating. Needless marital conflict, smothering stress, guilt, shame, and the inability to obey God's call are the results of living with unnecessary debt. When you face overdue bills, debt for non-necessities, and credit on non-appreciating items, you are on the road to financial bondage.

Cathy and I were married with little cash, but no debt. We lived very simply, refusing to go into debt for anything other than our first home.

Today we do keep a credit card (for convenient record keeping and the frequent flier miles we receive by using it), but it is paid off every month.

We have practiced an important financial principle: if we can't pay cash for it, we probably don't need it. If we do truly need it, God will provide it. He has over and over, time and again.

Many high-potential Christian leaders are defeated before they begin slowly crushing their lives and ministries with unmanageable debt. They never grow in their faith because they block God from providing for them. When they face a legitimate need they opt for the immediately easy, but ultimately painful path of accruing more debt.

In our church, we found that our potential leaders were freed to reach their potential after they worked through a class we offered on financial freedom. The victory came when each potential leader laid out an intentional plan to get out of debt, stay out of debt, and start tithing.

Is your debt load draining you of the time and energy you should be investing in your ministry?

2. Keep good records.

Be diligent to know the state of your flocks, and attend to your herds; for riches are not forever, nor does a crown endure to all generations (Proverbs 27:23-24).

When I was a boy, I watched my dad empty his pockets night after night. Each evening after dinner, he counted his change and recorded his expenses for the day. When we got married, Cathy and I kept a book where we wrote down every penny of income and "outgo." This helped us see our financial picture clearly each and every day, which shaped our priorities. Someone once stated a formula for financial disaster:

IGNORANCE + EASY CREDIT = CATASTROPHE

The money we have in this life is not ours. It belongs to our Master. We are simply managers of His resources. One day we will give an account of what we did with His money. It is our obligation to keep careful track of what He has given us. Let me encourage you to buy a budget book or use a software program in order to keep good financial records.

3. Plan your "outgo."

The plans of the diligent lead surely to plenty, but those of everyone who is hasty, surely to poverty (Proverbs 21:5).

Which sounds better to you: plenty or poverty? The verse above clearly states that financial planning leads to plenty, while haste (unplanned, impulsive buying) leads to poverty. Let me encourage you to plan your "outgo" in three important areas:

a) Determine how much you will *give.*

b) Determine how much you will *save.*

c) Determine how much you will *spend.*

Such a three-fold family financial plan is called a *budget.*

If keeping a budget sounds restrictive, let me assure you that it is not. A budget, if properly used, doesn't enslave you. It sets you free. It does not take money away from you; it gives you more money to use for what you want.

4. Spend wisely.

There is desirable treasure, and oil in the dwelling of the wise, but a foolish man squanders it (Proverbs 21:20).

When I was a nine-year old boy with a paper route, I discovered that I had a strong tendency to be an impulsive spender and someone who shops to cover emotional hurts. Impulsive spending is often the fastest road to financial bondage.

When we were first married, Cathy and I practiced three rules to curb impulsive spending:

• *Delayed action.* The bigger the purchase, the longer the delay before buying it.

• *Limited spending without marital discussion.* When we first got married, twenty-seven years ago, the amount was $20. Now it is $100.

• *Question the purchase.* We found that by asking a simple set of questions, we would ultimately be much happier with the things we did buy:

— Do we truly need it?

— Is the price reasonable?

— Can we substitute something less expensive for it?

— Have we shopped around?

— Will it put us into debt?

— Will it positively or negatively affect our spiritual life?

5. Be content with what you have.

Better is a little with the fear of the Lord, than great treasure with trouble. Better is a dinner of herbs where love is, than a fatted calf with hatred. Better is a dry morsel with quietness, than a house full of feasting with strife. Riches do not profit in the day of wrath, but righteousness delivers from death (Proverbs 15:16-17; 17:1; 11:4).

The goal here is to maintain a healthy and realistic view of money. Money should be viewed as a necessary tool and used skillfully in this life. One source of discontentment comes from struggling relationships, not from a lack of extra cash.

6. Honor God.

Honor the Lord with your possessions, and with the first fruits of all your increase; So your barns will be filled with plenty, and your vats will overflow with new wine (Proverbs 3:9-10).

Honoring God with our possessions means putting Him first. Elsewhere in the Old Testament this is expressed by giving God the first tenth (or tithe) of our income. I am not a legalist, but I am a fan of tithing. I found that by giving God the first tenth of my income makes three necessary and powerful statements:

• To God, I say thanks for past provisions.

• To others, I testify of my present priorities.

• To myself, I am demonstrating faith for future provisions.

I could tell you countless stories proving the fact that you cannot out-give God. But it would be better if you found out for yourself and wrote your own stories.

The "disease of me"

I have discovered that I am my biggest problem! God cannot bless or use me as He would like because I am in the way. No wonder Jesus repeatedly encouraged His followers to deny themselves.

Over the course of the last several years, God has repeatedly allowed circumstances in my life that test my true godly character and Biblical integrity versus what I think about myself. Let me offer you a set of questions that comprise "the disease of me." Each question has helped me see where I must make changes to gain the personal integrity required to lead effectively:

- How do I react when another is promoted over me, selected instead of me, or outshines me?
- How do I feel when others evaluate me as harshly as I evaluate or criticize myself?
- Do I think or speak too much about myself?
- Do I see everything in reference to myself?
- Am I able to listen to the praises of a rival without detraction, rebuttal, or belittling the person?
- Do I attach the affection of my followers more to the Christ within me than to myself?
- Do I give or accept exaggerated deference to or from other church leaders?
- Do I cling to authority too long?
- Am I actively training others to assume responsibility?
- Do I take myself, my successes, or my failures too seriously?
- Can I admit when I am wrong?
- Can I admit when I need to change?
- Can I laugh at myself and move on?

The best place to find healing from "the disease of me" is at the foot of the cross. Take some time and pray through the questions above. As you do, ask God to nail your pride and selfish ambition to the cross. The One who humbled Himself to give you the opportunity to make a difference is more than willing to take it.

Conclusion

In discussing the vital importance of strong character and personal integrity for the Christian leader, pastor and author, Stan Toler wisely observes, "Stellar achievement plus weak character equals disaster. Keep your character strong and your influence will be irresistible."[2]

Integrity is not created in a weekend. It is built through practicing spiritual disciplines and making wise decisions. Determine to become a leader of integrity through consistent self examination, self-discipline and self-reporting to a trusted accountability partner.

The Small Group Leader's PERSONAL INTEGRITY Worksheet

Do you have an accountability partner? If not, who could you ask?

How often do you or should you meet?

❑ Daily   ❑ Weekly   ❑ Every other week

What accountability questions do you or should you ask each other?

_____

_____

_____

Which of the three tests (morals, money, or me) do you struggle with most? Why?

_____

_____

_____

_____

_____

List three actions you plan to take to keep from being tripped up in the area of personal integrity (morals, money, or me):

1. _____

_____

_____

2. _____

_____

_____

3. _____

_____

_____

Chapter Three
PASSION

Joey is a new believer and the passionate leader of his small group of college-aged young men. Because of his passion to see his group and the guys in the group grow, he prays a lot, prepares well, invests deeply, and loves doing it. His group has grown and multiplied twice in the last three years.

Doug has been saved for a decade. Like Joey, he also leads a group for college-aged guys. He is leading the group because the original leader graduated and moved to another state. Doug prays a little, prepares minimally, and really only thinks about the group an hour or two before the meeting starts. His group has been steadily shrinking in size and he is not sure why.

The difference between Joey and Doug can be summarized in one word: *passion.*

A God-fueled passion is often overlooked by promising new leaders. Give me a leader with mediocre skills and great passion over one with great skills and no passion. He or she will turn a weekly meeting into a life-changing event. The passionate leader will spark others to action and keep going when others quit. It's no contest. Passion wins over skills every time.

Passion is more important than education, experience, or talent. Passion also makes up for a multitude of inadequacies. Passion is the fueling qualification of "high octane" spiritual leadership.

Are you passive or passionate about leading a small group?

Passion is heart and fire

When I write of a leader's passion, I am describing an "intense, driving, overmastering feeling or conviction." Passion is that which stirs the emotions, affections, devotions, and decisions of a leader or an organization. Passion provides an unrelenting sense of one's identity is and why he or she is alive. For you, it is the burning heart of a small group leader.

Although I am small in stature, I effectively played several sports and competed as a college athlete. Coaches often said that the only athletic tool I had was "heart." In other words, I had passion. I put all of myself into every play, every race, and every match. I practiced hard and played the game harder, mustering every ounce of energy I possessed.

Effective leaders pour their hearts out. They throw all of

themselves into what they are doing. They are not distracted, remaining focused on the moment to seize the opportunity.

As a kid, I heard preachers and coaches talk about the necessity of "having a fire in your belly." Passion is that fire in the belly that refuses to be quenched.

Passion is different than a goal, plan, or timeline. A goal describes what you are trying to accomplish. A plan describes how you intend to get there. A timeline answers when various aspects of the plan will be achieved. When you can put your passion on paper you answer the question, "Who am I and why am I here?"

Vision, goals, values, plans, and priorities are all very important. But knowing who you are and why you are here is even more important than knowing where you are going and how you intend to get there.

Passion in the "hood"

Pastor Andy Z. has succeeded where many others have failed. Twenty yeas ago, he went to one of the roughest neighborhoods in America to plant a multi-ethnic church. When I say rough, I mean *rough*. This inner city Chicago neighborhood ranks near the top in murder rates. Every time I have visited Andy I have heard gunshots.

Andy loves God and he loves the people in his "hood." His greatest strength as a leader is his unquenchable love for God and irresistible compassion for people. Within his heart blazes a relentless flame to reach the people in this area. This is his passion.

The last time I visited his church several adults were saved, including one homeless man. This poor fellow looked bad and smelled worse. He wore stained jeans, a torn sweatshirt, and soiled bird feathers pushed behind his ears into his afro. The sweatshirt he wore had a vulgar epitaph on the top. I learned they ministered to him for quite some time and he had not responded to the gospel before. Yet he did that morning.

As the homeless man was introduced to the congregation as a new child of God, my friend Andy ran forward, grabbed him and hugged him. And I mean he hugged him! Andy put his cheek right next to the filthy cheek of the homeless man. Andy held the man in his arms for several minutes and when they finally broke I saw tears running down both of their cheeks. The church burst into applause. That day, I felt God smiling.

Andy is making a difference in Chicago. That is his passion, and it shows.

What are you passionate about?

When bottled up, your passions can poison your joy. When released and untethered, your passions will change the world! Identifying what stirs deeply in your heart is an important step in understanding yourself and focusing your energy. It is an aid in maintaining motivation, enduring difficulties, and making wise decisions. An identified passion, or passions, is a vital tool in your leadership toolkit. Recognized and focused, your passions will give direction and drive to your ministry.

While all Christ-followers should be passionate about God and people, expressions of that passion vary from person to person. Your spiritual gifts, abilities, personalities, and experiences all play a part in the way you are wired for ministry. If you tap into them, these things will help determine and fuel your passions.

Some leaders are passionate about reaching the lost. Others burn to worship. Some are driven to intercession. Some leaders cannot keep from encouraging unity. For others, they are ablaze with the passion to dig into the Word of God and reveal its truths.

Are you passionate for unreached people groups in the 10/40 Window? Does your heart pound for the unchurched of North America? Some have a heart for the de-churched and others for "the chosen frozen." Do you weep over down-and-outers, or maybe up-and-outers? Maybe it is abused women, or alcoholic men, or people going through divorce, or material-obsessed yuppies. Your passion could be toward children or teens, college kids, young adults, senior adults, singles, couples, blended families, divorcees, or widows.

Maybe you love to organize, or serve behind the scenes, or care for the hurting, or challenge the complacent. Maybe you love to give to help the needy, or teach them how to solve their own problems. What are your passions?

Your ministry will be most effective and fulfilling when it is closely linked with your passions. Let me repeat that to drive it home. Your ministry will be most effective and fulfilling when it is most closely linked with your passions. For example, I have an undying passion for reaching the lost. So, the small groups I enjoyed leading have been those that are successful in reaching the lost. It did not matter if the group's focus was reaching teens or yuppies. As long as people got saved, I loved it! On the other hand, I once led a small group comprised of Christian senior adults who had no friends that needed Jesus. All their friends were saved and going to church somewhere. Within two months I was bored to tears.

If you love missions, make sure your group prays for missionaries and mission fields. Better yet, go on short-term mission trips together. If you have a heart of mercy for those who struggle with drugs or alcohol, start a group to help people break free of addiction. If you love the Word, invest the time during your small group meetings to dig into the Scriptures and apply what you find. Leading out of your passions makes leading a small group exciting and fulfilling.

Identify your passions

If you have difficulty identifying your passions, I suggest that you make it a matter of prayer and reflective thought. Over the years, I have accumulated several statements that often reveal what stirs one's heart. Thinking in terms of ministry, how would you complete each of the following statements?

If I had unlimited time, freedom and opportunity, I would . . .

I would die fulfilled if I could simply . . .

I always want to know more about . . .

I get very frustrated when I am not able to . . .

The one thing that I always go back to is . . .

When I am feeling confident I like to think about . . .

I usually sense God's blessing and anointing on my efforts in . . .

Write it down

I would be thrilled if you would complete this chapter with a simple statement of what you are most passionate about in terms of your life and ministry. A passion statement describes who you are and why you are here in one single, simple, memorable sentence. Examples of *general* passion statements are listed below:

To boldly go where no man has gone before!

To know Christ and make Him known.

To help ordinary people become extraordinary followers of Jesus Christ.

To love God and others with all my heart, soul, mind, and strength.

To win the lost at any cost.

When I was twenty years old, I wrote the following passion statement that helped me fuel and focus my decisions:

"To know, love and glorify God and be used of Him to reach as many people, as deeply as possible in the least amount of time."

As we raised three boys, Cathy and I crafted this parenting passion statement:

"To cooperate with God in raising godly Christian leaders who will make a difference."

As the lead pastor of a church, I led my church to adopt this passion statement:

To make a positive, eternal difference in Central Ohio and beyond through the local church.

Micro and macro passion statements

I often ask my pastoral students and pastors, "Who are you and why do you exist?" I enjoy watching them squirm to come up with the answer. As a professor, it is my job to help them wrestle through such issues. Until they do, their ministries will be unfocused and lacking in impact. Those who best align their ministries with their passions realize the greatest fulfillment and deepest impact.

Take a few minutes right now and jot down some possible statements that begin to capture your unique God-given passions. For example, my friend Randall has a life macro passion of: *"Living a life that reflects Christ in every step I take."* His daily micro passion statement under his life passion umbrella is: *"To reach people for Christ who don't have kids or who no longer have kids living at home in the Houston Heights."*

Below, write a macro passion statement expressing your life passion in one statement. Then, write a micro passion statement describing what you want to focus on and live out today.

My life's Macro Passion Statement:

_____

_____

_____

My life's Micro Passion Statement:

_____

_____

_____

What is the passion of your group?

I have found that the groups I lead do best when they have a clear passion statement. I have listed a few examples below.

To be an accepting place where unchurched students can meet God and grow in Him.

To reach people of various ethnic groups in a weekly gathering place which will show that the church is a beautiful mosaic of different peoples.

To intentionally gather spiritual seekers in a weekly meeting that will allow them to get their questions about Christianity answered in the context of community.

What is the passion for your group? As a group, who you are you and why do you exist? Write some possible passion statements for your group, based on what you have observed in the lives of your members:

_____

_____

_____

Turn Your Passions into SMART Objectives

Vague passions produce vague results. It is of little value to identify who you are and why you are here if you do not carry it to the next level and turn your passions into your goals and objectives. The "smarter" the objective, the greater the impact. A SMART objective is one that is specific, measurable, achievable, relevant, and time-bound.[1] (Peter Drucker, in his 1954 seminal work, "The Practice of Management" coined the usage of the acronym for SMART objectives.)

In this section I intend to help you turn your passions into SMART objectives. Take your macro and micro passion statements and create SMART objectives for each one.

Specific: Clearly determine exactly what you want to accomplish including as many details as possible.

Poor example: I am passionate about multiplication and I want our group to multiply.

Good example: To multiply my group, I will invest half an hour before our group meets every week mentoring my apprentice to effectively launch a new group with 6 others within a calendar year.

Measurable: Determine the measuring stick(s) for assessing your progress. Answer questions such as: How much? How many? How will I know when it is accomplished?

Poor example: I love the Word of God and want to read the Bible more.

Good example: I love the Word of God, therefore I will read the entire Bible in a year by reading three chapters from 10:00-10:20 p.m. each day.

Attainable: Create a goal that is achievable given your current situation, resources, knowledge, and time.

Poor example: Our small group is passionate about fulfilling the Great Commission and will multiply into ten new groups this month.

Good example: Our small group is passionate about fulfilling the Great Commission and will multiply into five new groups over the next ten years.

Relevant: Create goals that are closely aligned with your spiritual passions and purposes.

Poor example: Within one year, I will watch television for seventy straight hours to set a new world record.

Good example: My group members have stated they desire to be the hands and feet of Jesus in our community. Therefore, starting this week I will encourage our small group to feed the homeless once a month.

Time-Sensitive: Set times for achievement and deadlines for completing your goals.

Poor example: We love prayer. Therefore, our group will pray a lot.

Good example: We love prayer. Therefore, our group will pray together corporately fifteen minutes at the start of every group session and fifteen minutes with an accountability partner at the end of every group session for the next six weeks.

Write 'em down!

A Harvard Business School study found that 83% of the people in the United States do not have any clearly defined goals. 14% have goals, but their goals are not written down. Only 3% of the population has written goals.

The study also found that the 3% percent who maintained written goals were earning an astounding 10 times more than the 83% without goals![2] In addition, similar studies have shown that individuals with written goals maintain better health and enjoy happier marriages than those without goals.

Take the next few minutes and write down your life passions and SMART goals that plainly spell out your plan of action. While it may change drastically in the future as you review it and make modifications, at least you will have something in writing. You will discover that using this tool will help you stay on course and lead more powerfully.

The Small Group Leader's PASSION Worksheet

My Passion Statement(s):

Personal:

Family:

Small group:

My SMART Goals

Now, create at least one SMART goal for the key areas of your life.

My spiritual life:

My family life:

My small group:

Don't stop here. Share what you've written with your group!

Chapter Four
PURPOSE

Jason and Lisa have led a small group for three years. The first year was exiting. New people joined the group and new friendships were formed. The second year was also a joy. Michael and Abbie were raised up as new leaders, who multiplied a new group.

The third year produced little growth. Jason's job required more effort and keeping up with their three children distracted Lisa.

What was the root problem?

John, their small group coach, told them he thought they lost sight of their purpose. Lost purpose is a common cause of lethargic small groups.

Why Purpose?

A leader with purpose sees potential opportunities when others see obstacles. They see the possibilities of the future when others only see problems. They see the future before their followers, see further than their followers, and they see God in and through the whole process and the end product.

All of God's great leaders had a great purpose. Look at the list below. The reason these leaders changed history is because they had a big purpose and fulfilled their purpose:
• The purpose of Joseph was to feed the Egyptians during the famine.
• The purpose of Moses was to free God's people from Egypt.
• The purpose of Joshua was to possess the Promised Land.
• The purpose of David was to build God's house.
• The purpose of Nehemiah was to rebuild the walls of Jerusalem.
• The purpose of the early church was to preach Christ.
• The purpose of Paul was to take the gospel to the Gentiles.
• The purpose of Jesus was to seek and save the lost.

Purpose becomes a tool in the hands of effective leaders when it gets under their skin and stays there. All great accomplishments come when a group of followers are endued with the purpose of their leader. For example, the book of Nehemiah shows the power of purpose. The challenge of rebuilding the wall energized the workers (2:17-20), united the people and directed their efforts (Chapter 3), kept all of them going in the face of opposition (4:1-23; 6:1-4), and led to great accomplishment . . . they rebuilt the walls in a jaw-dropping 52 days (6:15)! Consider the first Christians. They ended up filling the entire city of Jerusalem with their teachings (Acts 5:28). Paul and his followers ended up turning the world upside down (Acts 17:6).

What is Purpose, Anyway?

A purpose is a big, overriding goal or objective. Some refer to it as a dream or a vision. Regardless of what you call it, it is an absolute essential for true leadership.

Vision, or purpose, is a picture of a preferred future told in the present. It is what could and should happen. It is a statement of faith as to what God can and will do. It is a need-meeting proposal that stretches others to greater sacrifice and impact. It is "a specific, detailed, customized, distinctive and unique notion of what you are seeking to do to create a particular outcome."[1]

Purpose can be differentiated from passion, priorities, plans, and goals:
• Passion explains why you exist.
• Priorities describe what is important.
• Plans tells how to get there.
• Goals are energizing mileposts marking progress along the way.

Your *purpose* describes where you are going.

How To Get Purpose

Purpose will come to you through several avenues. Let me suggest four keys to gaining and clarifying your purpose.

See the need

A great need inspires a great leader. Nehemiah purposed to rebuild the walls after being deeply affected by the need to do so (Neh. 1:2-11). Jesus was inspired to reach the multitudes by witnessing the needs of people who were weary and scattered like sheep with no shepherd (Matt. 9:35-38). Some leaders are inspired by need. Are you?

See the potential

Some leaders are more motivated by potential than by need. They get excited about what could be. They love the notion of doing something no one else has done yet. Does seeing the potential of your group do it for you?

Listen to God

Purpose is often born when we take the need and the potential to God in prayer. It is before God's throne that purpose is given for meeting the need and realizing the potential. Through prayer God's call becomes the leader's purpose.

Moses made it his life purpose to deliver God's people from slavery in Egypt to the Promised land. Joshua made it his life purpose to get the people established in the Promised Land. You must join these mighty leaders, aligning your purposes with God's purposes. You must listen to the still small voice of God and give everything you have to doing what He is doing.

"I get my vision from the Lord"

Recently I had the opportunity to meet with Pastor Sunday Adelaja. He is an incredible man of vision who is the Founder and Senior Pastor of The Embassy of the Blessed Kingdom of God for All Nations in Kiev, Ukraine. Sunday is a Nigerian-born leader in his mid-thirties, known as a dynamic communicator and church planter. He is widely regarded as the most successful pastor in Europe with over 25,000 members as well as daughter and satellite churches in 35 countries worldwide.

I asked him how and where he discovered his vision for such a remarkable ministry. His face lit up with a beautiful smile as he said, "I get my vision from the Lord. I spend one week every month alone with the Lord and His Word. It is there that He gives me His vision."

You may not be able to spend a week each month alone with the Lord, but you can still apply Pastor Sunday's approach. What if you spent an hour each week alone with the Lord seeking His vision for your life and group?

Ask probing questions

Often, a dream or purpose is not considered because it is thought to be impossible. Ask yourself two probing questions to clarify a purpose that is God-sized and "Him-possible" . . .

If I knew our group had no obstacles and unlimited resources, what would we love to do?

If I knew it was possible, what do I believe God would have us do?

Effective spiritual leaders learn how to receive a clear purpose of what the Lord wants to do with them and their ministries. They have learned that vision comes from the Lord. But it is rarely given immediately. Are you asking yourself and your group enough probing questions?

HOW TO USE PURPOSE TO LEAD MORE EFFECTIVELY

See it

One summer my son talked about launching a new group for high school students. Andrew and I spent time praying each day asking God what He had in mind for our group. He did not speak to us in an audible voice or through a mystical vision, but two pictures came to mind. First, we saw our house full of high school kids connecting with God every week. All types of kids were present, many meeting God for the first time. Second, we saw the group multiplying itself every year until groups were meeting all over our part of town.

To God's glory, this vision became a reality during Andrew's high school years. I firmly believe our vision was achieved because God conceived it within us and we possessed the faith to birth a powerful ministry.

State it as simply and specifically as possible

A good purpose statement can clarify and direct you and your group. It must be one or two sentences that are simple enough to be remembered, and specific enough to give direction. For example, the purpose statement for our group was, "To be a growing, prayer-saturated group where high school students gather weekly to meet with God and each other and to multiply at least once a year."

In the last chapter, we discussed using SMART goals to help you progress personally. Now, let me encourage you to motivate your group members through a purpose statement that is also specific, measurable, attainable, relevant, and time-oriented.

Specific

Your group's purpose statement (often called a vision statement) should state who is to be involved (i.e., high school students).

It should describe what you do together . . . gather weekly to meet with God and each other and to multiply at least every year.

It also describes what will be key elements of making that happen . . . a growing, prayer-saturated group.

Measurable

For our high school group, we answered these five questions of measurement (I call them "measurables") each week:

1) Did we saturate the group with prayer?
2) Did new people visit this week?
3) Did we meet with God?
4) Did we have positive fellowship with each other?
5) Are we taking steps toward multiplying in a year?

Attainable

Good purpose statements are stretching, but not too far out of reach. Your statement should be attainable, but require everything your group has within it to see it become a reality.

For my group, I can say we attained the middle three measurable questions above: new people visited most weeks, we met with God regularly, and we enjoyed positive fellowship with one other. We were lax on the first and last ones: saturating our group with prayer and taking steps toward multiplying once a year.

As a result, we failed to multiply the last year we led that group. While we were successful overall, we could have been far *more* successful if we remained focused to experience all five "measurables" every week.

Relevant

A good purpose statement conveys elements of the deep desires of everyone on your leadership team or group. It meets needs in your community. Ensure your purpose statement makes a difference in the lives of others beyond your group and its members.

Time-oriented

Our high school group's purpose statement was, "to multiply at least once a year." Stating a defined timeframe is important. It not only speaks of multiplication, but it gives a date for accomplishing it. Stating "once a year" was a challenge for my group, yet it was an attainable time frame.

You will undoubtedly revisit your purpose statement to refine it. You may change it to be more specific about reaching the lost, or the number of leaders you will train, or the number of lost people you hope to reach within a specified time frame.

Try it right now. Write a tentative version of a purpose statement for your small group that is SMART:

_____

_____

_____

_____

_____

Share it with key people

By talking about the purpose with key people in your group, it creates "buy in" or adoption. As this happens, expect them to add their own nuances to your purpose statement. This is a good sign of progress.

For example, before launching our group for high school kids, Andrew and I had just returned from a few days of prayer-saturated ministry at a Christian university. He added to our purpose statement that the group should be saturated in prayer, and he volunteered to lead a prayer gathering each week before the group meeting.

Then, we began to cast the vision (our group's purpose) to the people we were recruiting to join our leadership team. My wife, Cathy, bought in by agreeing to host the group and added to the vision the desire to make the group very biblical (since kids in our culture know so little about the Bible).

One of our adult apprentices wanted our group to have definite direction so that it was not a waste of time. Another of my sons, Daniel, bought in, stressing a desire to see lost kids find salvation and join the group. One of the ladies we spoke with was captured with the idea of using the group to develop the girls into leaders. Another student joined our leadership team just because he thought it would be fun.

In two weeks, the purpose of a multiplying high school group had gone from the vision of Andrew and myself to the purpose owned by several others. It had become "the dream of a team."

Because others owned it by adding to it, they worked hard to make it succeed . . . and it did! Within four months we had grown to almost 45 students meeting each week in six smaller break-out groups throughout our home. In week seventeen, we sent a dozen off to meet in a second location. Within a year, our original group had grown to 60 students meeting in eight groups throughout my house and had multiplied a third group. Sharing the purpose statement and encouraging others to add to it made the difference!

Share it Often

When should the vision be communicated? At every opportunity!

Purpose is only powerful to the extent that it is shared. Too often leaders define their dream, but fail to reach it simply because they do not spend enough time sharing their dream with others. The purpose will not accomplish all that it can unless it is shared. It won't attract followers or produce leaders. It can't compel action or build morale. It won't give a sense of direction. It can't inspire resolve and encourage sacrifice unless and until it is shared. *It Also Need Participation OF the Leader!*

It just makes sense. A good purpose that is frequently shared will always accomplish more than a great vision that is rarely shared. People must hear the dream described often enough to be able to recite it. They must have the picture painted for them so frequently that they know what it means and where they fit into it. If they hear it often enough to adopt it as their own, they will share it with others.

Leaders who are successful at multiplying their groups describe the purpose of the group week after week as reaching out and multiplying. Leaders often fail because they do not describe the vision often enough. Because they get tired of hearing themselves state it, they wrongly assume others are tired of hearing it. Not so!

Share it in as many ways as possible

There are many mediums in which to share your dream. Effective ways of sharing the dream include: story-telling, slogans, signs or banners, or even songs that promote it. Publicly teach on it, pray about it, and note any progress in fulfilling it. Write about it in a letter, refer to it in a conversation, and mention it in a testimony. Your effectiveness increases dramatically by employing multiple means of communicating your dream.

Let me share one last bit of advice. There is something powerful about looking someone in the eye and sharing with passion and confident humility that God is going to do great things in and through your small group. Do not overlook the power of a private conversation to share the purpose of your group.

The goal is clear. Find your purpose as a leader. When it is written down and shared with others consistently, you will be effectively using yet another power tool for small group leadership.

Your Personal PURPOSE Worksheet

What is your purpose in life? Write it below:

List the people with whom you want to share it . . .

List the various ways you will creatively share it with others . . .

The Effective Small Group Leader's PURPOSE Worksheet
(Excellent questions to use in your next meeting)

What is God's purpose for our group beyond ministering to one another and meeting together each week?

How can it be stated in one simple, specific sentence? (Write it below)

What must we do to ensure we are reminded of it weekly? List the ideas offered by group members here:

Chapter Five
PRIORITIES

What really matters? What are the most important things in your life? One way to determine your priorities is to consider what you want people to say about you at your funeral or write on your headstone. Epitaphs are brief statements commemorating or epitomizing a deceased person. They can be spoken or written. They are pithy statements that attempt to summarize a person's life. Some are serious while others are not. In years past, they often were written on gravestones. Over the years I have visited numerous cemeteries and checked other sources for epitaphs. A couple of my favorites include:

A cemetery head stone in Ribbesford, England, reads:
> *The children of Israel wanted bread*
> *and the Lord sent them manna.*
> *Old clerk Wallace wanted a wife,*
> *and the Devil sent him Anna.*

In a Uniontown, Pennsylvania cemetery one gravestone tells the story of an automobile accident:
> *Here lies the body of Jonathan Blake.*
> *Stepped on the gas instead of the brake.*

A head stone in a Silver City, Nevada cemetery tells of a gun battle:
> *Here lays Butch, We planted him raw.*
> *He was quick on the trigger, But slow on the draw.*

Some don't rhyme but are equally good. I love the words on Margaret Daniel's grave at Hollywood Cemetery in Richmond, Virginia:
> *She always said her feet were killing her*
> *but nobody believed her.*

I also get a big kick out of this gravestone in a Thurmont, Maryland cemetery:
> *Here lies an Atheist.*
> *All dressed up and no place to go.*

My favorite is one we saw on vacation at a cemetery in Key West, Florida:
> *I told you I was sick!*

Those are all funny. But the best *serious* headstone I have ever seen tells of a man whose life made a positive difference. Dr. John Geddie went to the remote island of Aneityum in 1848 and worked there for God for 24 years as a missionary. On the tablet erected to his memory, these words were inscribed:

> *When he landed in 1848, there were no Christians.*
> *When he left in 1872, there were no heathen.*[1]

What would someone write as an epitaph of your life?

Several years ago, a friend of mine was diagnosed with cancer and died soon after. His family held a service celebrating his life. During the service his family and friends shared the positive impact he left on their lives. After that night, I determined to make sure I knew what was most important and vowed to invest the rest of my life living for what mattered most.

Let me ask you: Are you living for that which is most important? What do you want people to say about you at your funeral? What do you want God to say to you at the Bema judgment seat?

The key to being prepared for the end is creating priorities in the present. Every optimally effective person and high impact spiritual leader makes setting priorities a prime concern. They learn to say "no" to the good in order to say a much stronger "yes" to the best!

Intensify your concentration in order to maximize your impact

When I was a boy, I enjoyed holding a magnifying glass over an earthworm that made the mistake of crawling across the sidewalk. The rays of the sun were concentrated and magnified through the glass to such a level of intensity that it burned holes in the unsuspecting worm. We thought it was fun. The worm? Not so much.

Lasers work much the same way. They emit light in a tightly focused wavelength. A sharply focused, high powered laser can cut through steel.

Many Christian leaders have minimal impact in ministry because they are spread thinly over a broad area, much like a common light bulb. Without an intentional concentration on your priorities, you'll never have the powerful ministry you deserve.

Narrow your focus

A few years ago I consulted a church that was in a death spiral. Even though they were in the middle of one of the fastest growing areas of their state, they had suffered a steady decline for ten straight years. If the decline continued, this church would be forced to close its doors.

Although they had more than one obstacle to overcome, one problem was glaringly evident. They had dozens of ineffective committees. Each member was on several, spending their week nights in meetings instead of doing ministry. My advice was to prioritize. Shut down all committees for one year and invest that time "loving your neighbors" and in small groups ministering to one another.

After thirty years of being a leader and training leaders, I am convinced that the failure to prioritize is one of the most dangerous traps churches and leaders face. Leaders are good-hearted, active people who find themselves involved in too many things. In order to make an impact, a world-changing leader must narrow their focus, do a few things well, and live by priorities.

PRIORITIZE OR AGONIZE!

There are many disappointments that come when you fail to prioritize. These include: missing out on living for that which is most important, eternal, and productive; failing to overcome overload; surrendering to the dragon of disorganization; and self-sabotaging your life and leadership.

Church leaders are overloaded

When was the last time you said, "I'm too busy," or "I'm too tired," or "I just don't have enough time," or "I don't have enough energy?"

What's the problem? We're overloaded. We have more information, more things, more debt, more expectations, more changes, and more options than ever before. Do you really think God made us to live this way? I don't think so.

Many small group leaders live with the frustration of ministry fatigue and the sabotage of self-inflicted stress. We are not merely working, we are *overworked*. It's not a matter of being committed to ministry either. We over-committed. Christian leaders today are flat-out exhausted.

Each of us has physical, emotional, financial, and mental thresholds that must remain in check. Once these thresholds are exceeded, the result is painful. For example, physical or emotional overload can lead to anxiety, hostility, resentment, depression, sickness, and breakdowns.

Overload occurs when the requirements upon us exceed what we are able to bear. Camels carry great loads. However, if a camel is already maximally loaded the addition of a mere straw will break its back. The straw didn't break its back . . . the entire load was to blame.

Sociologist Alvin Toffler observed that researchers strongly agree on two principles. The first is that man has a limited capacity. The second is that when man's capacity is exceeded, it leads to serious breakdown in performance. Instead of doing one ministry well, many small group leaders dabble ineffectively in several areas to be helpful, feel needed, or because they hate to say "no."

What is the solution to the anguish of overload? Prioritize!

Are you disorganized?

Maybe you aren't overloaded, but are just disorganized . . . or worse, both. What does disorganization look like? I jotted down a few indicators:
• My desk is cluttered.
• I leave a trail of forgotten appointments, unanswered phone messages, my email in-box is overflowing, and I miss deadlines.
• My car is dirty inside and out and behind in scheduled maintenance.
• I find myself wasting time on small, non-priority tasks.
• My level of productive work is not what it could or should be.
• I am late to meetings and events.
• I feel under-prepared.
• My time with the Lord has suffered.
• My relationships show signs of strain.

I find that if more than one of these things is true in my life, I am disorganized and feeling overloaded. How many are currently in your life?

Are you guilty of living for "the less important?"

I doubt that anyone reading this book would stand before Jesus after they die and hear Him say that they had lived a bad life. I also doubt that many of us would hear Him tell us that we lived a life focused on the absolutely most important things. Often, we are guilty of living for the less important things. We choose to do a lot of good activities to the exclusion of the very best.

Prioritizing to greater productivity

The people who are viewed as most successful in life are those who have learned to prioritize. Who hasn't heard the name of Tiger Woods? He is a prime example of one who has laser-focused his energy into the competitions that matter most. Insatiable golf fans and television producers would love to see Tiger play every PGA tournament. But Tiger plays fewer tournaments over the course of the year than his PGA brethren and champions such as Arnold Palmer and Jack Nicklaus. His focus is on the four majors: the Masters, British Open, U.S. Open, and PGA Championship. They are his priority. While he does not apologize for passing up tournaments of lesser prestige, Tiger's practice regimen and self discipline surrounding preparation for the majors are legendary.

Could he tally up additional wins and earn even more prize money if he played more? Probably. But that's not a priority for Tiger. Not only are the other tournaments less important for his definition of success, but they would be a distraction in the pursuit of his ultimate goal: winning as many majors as possible.

Essentially, Woods has determined that focusing only on the events that are the most important will allow him to reap the greatest benefit. The lesson is simple but powerful . . .

The quality of your impact often matters more than the quantity of your activities. Some activities are simply more productive than others.

Realities about Priorities

Everything cannot *be a priority.* T.V. commercials I've seen recently state, "You can have it all!" Don't believe it. You are not an infinite being and limited in capacity. You cannot have it all or do it all without sacrifice. If you were to embrace everything, you would become overloaded and serious, life-changing problems would arise.

Everything shouldn't *be a priority.* Very few activities qualify as the best or are a true priority. You must choose carefully when it comes to your priorities.

How will you know what is a true priority? I use the following three criteria for establishing my priorities in life and ministry:

1. Importance: Some activities and investments are more important than others. Jesus was the Master of all things, including living a well-managed life. He simplified life for us into one awesome statement recorded in Matthew 22:37-40:

> *You shall love the LORD your God with all your heart, with all your soul, and with all your mind. This is the first and great commandment. And the second is like it: You shall love your neighbor as yourself. On these two commandments hang all the Law and the Prophets.*

This passage is powerful for two reasons among many. First, relationships are given as most important (loving God and loving people). Second, Jesus does not mention achievements, careers, incomes, money, possessions, power, popularity, pleasure, entertainment, or recreation. According to Jesus' words above, we must make God and other people our top priorities. Consider your answers to each of the questions below before you read any further. The answers will help you understand what is currently most important to you.

• What are your essentials?
• What are your "non-negotiables?"
• What are the most important things in your life?
• Are you investing your life in God and people?

2. Eternality: Some activities and investments are more lasting than others. Again it is Jesus who simplifies life when he tells us to remember that some things are more lasting than others. From Matthew 6:19-21 we read:

> *Do not lay up for yourselves treasures on earth, where moth and rust destroy and where thieves break in and steal; but lay up for yourselves treasures in heaven, where neither moth nor rust destroys and where thieves do not break in and steal. For where your treasure is, there your heart will be also.*

Through a careful study of God's Word, I've found five investments that are eternal in nature:

• God (Deuteronomy 33:27)
• People's Souls (John 5:28 -29)
• God's Word (Isaiah 40:8)
• Prayers (Revelation 5:6-8)
• True Fellowship (Malachi 3:16)

Interestingly, a healthy small group focuses on each of those five eternal investments. They worship God, strategize to evangelize the lost, dig into and apply God's Word, spend quality time in prayer, and experience true fellowship. Let me ask you an important question. What percentage of your life is invested in that which will yield an eternal return? How about your small group?

3. Productivity: Some activities and investments are more productive than others. An Italian economist named Vilfredo Pareto observed that 80% of income in Italy went to 20% of the population. Business management thinker Joseph Juran saw a universal application to Pareto's law which he called the Pareto principle. It is also known as the *80-20 rule*, the *law of the vital few*, or the *principle of factor sparsity*. It states that, for many events, 80% of the effects comes from 20% of the causes. It is a common rule of thumb in business: "80% of your sales comes from 20% of your clients."

Pareto's principle applies to churches as well:

- 20% of the sermon yields 80% of the benefit to those hearing it.
- In most churches, 20% of the church members do 80% of the work and financial giving.
- 20% invite 80% of the guests.
- 20% of the members take up 80% of the pastor's time in counseling.
- 20% of the membership provides 80% of the leadership for a church.
- In most churches, 20% of the programs and ministries yield 80% of the impact and spiritual fruit.
- 20% of the members eat 80% of the food at church-wide pot lucks!

If you were to make a list of ten things you need to get done sooner than later, you'll discover the principle is at play in your life as well. Two of those items will probably make a far bigger impact if completed compared to the other eight *combined*. The art of prioritizing is learning to choose the top two by categorizing them as problems, pests, procrastinators, or producers.

PROBLEMS — *Activities that are urgent and important.*

For example, if your son is nauseas, you have a problem. Get a bowl. If the house is on fire, you have a problem. Call 911! If the final exam is one hour from now and you have yet to study for it, you have a problem. Start praying for the rapture! If your car breaks down in the middle of the interstate during rush hour because you forgot to check the oil level, you have a problem. Call a tow truck. No one wants to live a life plagued with problems like these.

PESTS — *Activities that are urgent, but not important.*

A pest is when the phone rings with someone wanting to sell you replacement windows when you live in an apartment. Or, it's junk Email crowding out important notes from friends or business associates.

People can be pests too. Starved for attention, certain individuals constantly ask you to drop everything and help them with something that is not a genuine crisis.

PROCRASTINATORS — *Activities that are not urgent and not important.*

These issues take time away from that which is really important. Most of what is on television can be categorized a procrastinator. Much of the web surfing we do fits the definition of a procrastinator. Relaxing in front of the TV or surfing the web isn't terrible by any means, but when these activities become a greater priority over producers described below, the person is in serious trouble and doesn't yet realize it!

PRODUCERS — *Activities that are not urgent but very important.*

Praying with your children when they are tots isn't urgent, but it's very important. Reading your Bible is rarely urgent, but is lasting. Turning off the TV or computer to have a meaningful conversation with your spouse or children isn't always urgent, but is very important. Prioritizing Sunday worship isn't urgent for many, but it has eternal ramifications. Changing the oil in your car, sharing your faith with a friend, saving instead of spending, exercising regularly, and giving your worries to God through prayer are all non-urgent things that serve as preventative medicine.

If you don't "prioritize your producers," they will turn into problems sooner than later. (I invest my time on producers because I hate to deal with problems as described on the previous page.)

A TOOL FOR DETERMINING PRIORITIES

Steven Covey developed a four-quadrant view of activities. The top grid pictured to the right shows the four realms of activities. Every activity you will engage in today will either involve dealing with what I refer to as a *problem*, handling a *pest*, engaging in a *procrastinator*, or investing in a *producer*.

How to establish your priorities
- *Evaluate.* Pick your top priorities considering importance, eternity, and productivity.
- *Eliminate.* Determine the activities and investments that should not be priorities in your life.
- *Estimate.* Select the activities and investments that best reflect good priorities (they are eternal, important, or productive) for the next three weeks, the next three months, the next three years, and the next thirty years.
- *Activate.* Plug these producing priorities into your monthly calendar, weekly schedule, daily to do list, etc.

Consider the activities that usually crowd your schedule. Write a few into the appropriate blocks in the grid provided:

More Important

	Problems	Producers	
	1.	1.	**N**
U	2.	2.	**O**
R	3.	3.	**T**
G	Pests	Procrastinators	**U**
E			**R**
N	1.	1.	**G**
T	2.	2.	**E**
	3.	3.	**N**
			T

Less Important

Now, consider the activities that occupy most of your group's time. Write them into the appropriate blocks in the grid given below.

More Important

	Problems	Producers	
	1.	1.	**N**
U	2.	2.	**O**
R	3.	3.	**T**
G	Pests	Procrastinators	**U**
E			**R**
N	1.	1.	**G**
T	2.	2.	**E**
	3.	3.	**N**
			T

Less Important

By categorizing your personal and small group priorities with this grid system, you will clearly see what to focus on . . . and more importantly, *why* you should focus on that priority.

The Effective Small Group Leader's PRIORITIES Worksheet

Effective leaders avoid the trap of merely doing more. They learn to do fewer things more effectively. Take a few minutes and pick your top priorities.

List Ten, Pick Two

1. Select an area of your small group (outreach, worship, fellowship, service to the community, study of the Word, prayer, and so on).

2. List ten things that need to be done in that area:

_____

_____

_____

_____

_____

_____

_____

_____

_____

_____

_____

_____

_____

_____

_____

_____

_____

_____

_____

3. Now select the top two priorities and circle them.

4. Write a short description of how you will focus on each one by doing them first and doing them well:

_____

_____

_____

_____

_____

_____

_____

_____

_____

_____

_____

Learn to do the same with your church, family, week, month, year, and decade. You will see dramatic changes in your life! This is one powerful tool for a leader, isn't it?

Chapter Six
PLANNING

"Plan your work and work your plan." I would be surprised if you have not heard this before. The question is, do you do it?

I am honored to teach and train hundreds of young people who possess strong ministry aspirations. Most have big dreams. However, many are still so young they have little or no idea how to turn those dreams into reality.

I also have the awesome privilege of training small group leaders, church planters, pastors, and missionaries. I am amazed at how many permit the pressures of day-to-day life and ministry to take them off course, pushing them onto a rocky path of ineffectiveness. Because they violate basic leadership principles, everyone involved in their ministries is frustrated. In each case, the ministry they oversee and serve is failing to reach its potential.

A few leaders I train are just the opposite. They keep plowing ahead with their plan of action, refusing to be dissuaded from finishing what they set out to do. I call it "planning and perspiring." These men and women are leaders who are also making an impact in unlikely settings with limited resources.

This chapter presents both essential sides of the leadership sword . . . planning your work and working your plan. Work without planning leads to wasted energy. Planning without work leads to aborted dreams and regrets. You must do both!

PLANNING

"Cruise to Nowhere"

I have ministered in several churches in Florida's coastal towns. Recently I saw a sign that intrigued me. It said, "Cruise to nowhere!" My hosts explained that on a "cruise to nowhere" people get on board a cruise ship, leave the pier, go out to sea, and travel in circles for several days. Those onboard enjoy several days of resort living as they dine on sumptuous meals, lounge around the pool working on their tan, enjoy the shows, and participate in other onboard activities.

"Cruising to nowhere" may be a great vacation, but it makes for a miserable life. Many small groups and churches are little more than cruises to nowhere because they do not have a plan of action. In order to gain a sense of fulfilment, your life, family, small group, business, and church needs direction.

Planning is the rudder that puts you on "a cruise to somewhere." Don't waste the opportunities God has given you by drifting aimlessly in circles. Lead your group to do something great for the kingdom with purpose and planning.

Planning is looking ahead

"Planning is bringing the future into the present so that you can do something about it now."[1] Because planning is looking ahead, it is foundational to effective leadership. If you want people to follow you, you must know where you are going and how to get there. I agree with Leroy Eims who wrote, "A leader is one who sees more than others see, who sees further than others see, and sees before others see."[2]

Just to clarify what has been covered in previous chapters, let me reiterate that your *purpose* states where you want to go and your *passion* explains why you want to go there. Planning spells out how you plan to get there. Planning is creating a map for a desired future.

Leadership is more than just steering the ship. A helmsman keeps his hand at the wheel and takes orders as to when to turn the wheel. The captain charts the course. Effective leadership uses the tool of planning to determine the best course to reach their destination.

Planning is preparing to succeed

Benjamin Franklin, one of the founding fathers of the United States, was also a leading printer, satirist, political theorist, politician, scientist, inventor, civic activist, statesmen, and diplomat. He also published "Poor Richard's Almanac." In between each dated calendar page, he sprinkled his various bits of wisdom including:

"Time is money."

"Fish and visitors stink in three days."

"There are no gains without pains."

"One today is worth two tomorrows."

"Have you somewhat to do tomorrow, do it today."

"Sloth, like rust, consumes faster than labor wears, while the used key is always bright."

"Early to bed, and early to rise, makes a man healthy, wealthy, and wise."

Most importantly for our discussion, Franklin also noted this saying: "By failing to prepare, you are preparing to fail."

Planning saves time

Business experts claim that every minute an individual spends planning their goals, activities, and time saves ten minutes of work in the execution of those plans. Read that again. One minute of planning saves ten minutes of doing. Wow!

This means cautious advance planning will yield a return of 1,000% on your investment of mental, emotional, and physical energy. Therefore, spending a meaningful period of time reflecting on your strategy and goals *before* taking action is always a smart move.

Planning maximizes one's time

You are busy and don't have extra time to waste. Planning helps you use the time you have most effectively. You may think you don't have time to develop a plan, but it's the other way around . . . you don't have enough time to do it over. It has to be done right the first time if at all possible.

Life is not a dress rehearsal. You get one shot at life. It is up to you to make the most of it. If you don't, you will never get the chance to get it back or try it again. Planning helps you use your time wisely.

HOW TO PLAN

Planning is not complicated. A good plan takes into consideration only three major issues:

Destination: Where do we want to go? (This is the big objective or the primary purpose.)

Present Location: What is our current situation? What is the gap between the real and the ideal? Why is there a gap? What are our current strengths and weaknesses, helping and hindering forces, and available resources?

Road Map: How do we intend to reach our hoped for destination? (This is the route that is to be taken. Taking into account strengths and weaknesses, helping and hindering forces, and available resources, the road map provides the progressive steps of the plan.)

Planning for personal and ministry growth

As a young leader I realized that personal growth would be required to see my small group grow. I admitted that I must make radical changes if I hoped to reach my potential. With this in mind, I put together a personal growth plan. It was developed as follows:

Destination/the major objective: Become the type of leader God could trust to lead a multiplying small group.

Present Situation: I led a stagnant small group that had lost momentum and not multiplied in several years.

Road Map: I broke my plan into two parts…

General Objective: I must become a leader of leaders. I must spend dedicated time adopting leadership principles into my life so I can in turn pour them into potential leaders.

Specific Steps: I will commit the next few years of my life to the following activities:

1. Listen to a leadership or small group ministry podcast or CD each week.
2. Read one leadership book a month.
3. Spend time before group each week meeting with my small group apprentices to share what I am learning.
4. Give my apprentices specific things to do each week (pray for group members, contact absentees, plan social or outreach activities, lead the ice breaker, or facilitate the discussion).
5. Set a date to multiply and work toward it.
6. Talk and pray about multiplication in group every week.

My results

The first few months that I worked my plan, I didn't see great strides. In many ways, I was plowing and planting. But I was slowly changing, and my group began to change too. It took many weeks, but my small group developed multiplication skills and recaptured a multiplication mind set.

At month six, I saw noticeable changes. Our group grew from 10 to 18 in regular attendance. My apprentices caught the vision, excited about the growth and potential of the group to form new groups. At twelve months we had successfully multiplied into two healthy groups, and both groups were "pregnant" with new apprentices.

WHEN PLANNING IS NOT ENOUGH

$100\% \Rrightarrow 67\% \Rrightarrow 10\% \Rrightarrow 2\%$

According to some experts, only sixty-seven out of 100 people set goals for themselves. Of those sixty-seven, only ten have made plans to achieve them. Of those ten, only *two* take action to make their dreams realities.

Who are these triumphant few? Those who take action!

Someone noticed that the only place where "success" comes before "work" is in the dictionary. It is not enough to plan your work. You must also work your plan. The greatest plans in the world won't work if you don't.

Successful spiritual leaders not only have God-given dreams and carefully laid plans, they take action to see those plans become a reality.

99% perspiration

Thomas Edison was an American inventor and businessman who developed the phonograph and the long lasting light bulb. This tireless worker authored an astounding 1,093 U.S. patents.

Edison modeled the power of perspiration. He failed 10,000 times before finally discovering the right materials to make the incandescent light bulb burn brightly and last. Think about that . . . 10,000 times! He often said, "Genius is one percent inspiration, and ninety-nine percent perspiration."

Few of us have the intellect to qualify as geniuses, but all of us can be hard workers. Without exception, effective small group leaders work at it and sweat a lot. High impact spiritual leadership does not happen by accident. It occurs as a result of careful planning combined with hard work. If you create a plan of action for yourself and your group—working hard to achieve it for as long as it takes—you will succeed.

The answer is hard work

Joel Comiskey surveyed 700 small group leaders in eight distinct cultures to unlock the "secrets" of multiplying small groups. He writes, "I discovered that the potential to lead a growing, successful small group does not reside with the gifted, the educated, or those with vibrant personalities. The answer rather is hard work."[3]

I spoke with Joel several months ago about the key characteristics of successful small group leaders. He said that all of his research revealed that multiplying small leaders really had only two common denominators: prayer and diligence.[4]

I agree wholeheartedly with Joel and his research. Many talented leaders have failed because they were either distracted or unmotivated to work hard. On the other hand, many ordinary leaders have experienced extraordinary results because they were willing to put in the hard work necessary to succeed.

The Common Denominator of Success

At a 1940 convention for insurance agents, Albert Gray delivered what was to become a famous address. His talk, "The Common Denominator of Success" has been turned into a pamphlet that has circulated around the globe. Gray summarized his findings in one sentence:

> The common denominator of success—the secret of success of every man who has ever been successful—lies in the fact that he formed the habit of doing things that failures don't like to do.

In explaining his meant he stated:

> Perhaps you have wondered why it is that our biggest producers seem to like to do the things that you don't like to do. They don't! And I think this is the most encouraging statement I have ever offered to a group of life insurance salesmen. But if they don't like to do these things, then why do they do them? Because by doing the things they don't like to do, they can accomplish the things they want to accomplish. Successful men are influenced by the desire for pleasing results. Failures are influenced by the desire for pleasing methods and are inclined to be satisfied with such results as can be obtained by doing things they like to do.

As is true in anything else, successful small leaders are those who work hard at the things other small leaders avoid. They contact small members regularly. They invite new people. They pray for their group members. They plan a weekly small group agenda and a small group activity calendar. They do all the things they know they should do, but usually don't get around to doing.

Effective leaders do what they need to do and learn to enjoy it. They become totally engrossed in small group leadership. They are successful because they have learned to love what they are doing. They don't love it because it is easy or because everything always goes according to plan. They learn to love it because they know they are making a difference in people's lives, an eternal difference.

As you develop a plan of action and work your plan with others in your group, you will see incremental change. Success comes one small victory at a time. Be patient with the process and celebrate the small advances toward the goals you have set. In this chapter I wrote of my story of success, which took time and hard work. You too will have a story of success to share with others if you plan for success and work that plan.

The Effective Small Group Leaders PLANNING Worksheet

First, make a plan for personal development. Where would you like to be five years from now? What about you needs to change? What must be done in order for you to get there?

My Plan for Personal Development

5 year destination: (List one major objective to accomplish.)

_____

_____

_____

_____

_____

Describe your present situation: (List current strengths and weaknesses, helping and hindering forces, and available resources.)

_____

_____

_____

_____

_____

Road Map: (Write out the steps you know you must take to accomplish your objective in the next five years. Be specific!)

_____

_____

_____

_____

_____

_____

_____

_____

_____

_____

_____

Where would you like your small group to be in the next 12 months? How many groups could be birthed out of your group in the next two years? What must change to see these things happen? What should be done to achieve the objectives?

My Plan for Small Group Ministry Development

Small group destination: (List one major objective to accomplish.)

_____

_____

_____

_____

_____

Describe your group's present situation: (List current strengths and weaknesses, helping and hindering forces, and available resources.)

_____

_____

_____

_____

_____

Road Map: (Write out the steps you know you and your group must take to accomplish your objectives. Be specific!)

_____

_____

_____

_____

_____

_____

_____

_____

_____

_____

Chapter Seven

PEOPLE SKILLS

Tommy and Doris are very faithful and committed small group leaders who love God. They are passionate about worship and prayer, and dig deep into the Word of God each week. They just don't like people as much compared to these things . . . and it shows! Their group is stagnant and they're losing members.

Bret and Lisa are also very faithful and committed small group leaders who love God. They are passionate about worship and prayer, and dig deep into the Word of God. But unlike Tommy and Doris, Bret and Lisa have placed a high value on people. Their small group mushroomed with new members and multiplied twice in the past three years.

Christian leadership is all about people. Without people, there is no one to lead. Goals, plans, projects, worship, and Bible study are important, but only to the extent that they help people find personal transformation.

By nature, I am more of a project person than a people person. But I learned that leadership effectiveness is closely tied with my ability to build significant relationships with people. As the Chinese proverb states, "He who thinks he is leading when no one is following is only taking a walk."

Small groups ministry is a great indicator of effectiveness with people. Simply put, if people don't like you, they won't come to your house. Beyond that, if you don't effectively love people, you won't be able to positively influence them.

Relational banking

Relationships are just like bank accounts. Realize it or not, you have a relational account with every person within your sphere of influence. Every positive interaction makes a deposit in that account. Every negative dealing with a person creates a withdrawal in that relational account.

Influencing others comes easily when there is a positive balance in one's relational accounts. You will always struggle to influence people when there is little or no equity in your relationship.

Small group leaders who practice good people skills continually make positive installments into others. Then, when they need to call a member to make a change or challenge them to a new level of commitment to God and the group, the member is willing to follow.

Effective leaders have mastered the art of relational banking. They constantly think of ways to make deposits in the lives of the people around them. They are not only well liked; they are easily followed. These leaders understand that effective ministry runs on the train track of healthy relationships and thrives in the atmosphere of positive relational investment.

How leaders make relational deposits

The Bible supplies the clearest guidelines for how to get along well with people. Leaders can improve their people skills immediately by obeying the "one another" commands found in the New Testament. Let's look at a few that will provide immediate help to your relationships:

Use greetings to make others feel important.
(Romans 16:16; *"Greet one another with a holy kiss"* (Romans 16:16). (See also 1 Cor. 16:20; 2 Cor. 13:12; 1 Peter 5:14.)

Relational deposits are made every time one person makes another person feel valued and appreciated. Effective leaders move out of their comfort zone to greet people warmly.

In the first century church, an appropriate greeting was a kiss. Today, a good greeting may be a handshake or a hug. Let me make one thing perfectly clear: I am not advocating giving everyone you meet a great big smooch on the lips! However, wise leaders use a greeting for an emotional deposit.

Connecting with people is really very simple. But if you are an introvert like me, it is good to review the basics. A greeting that makes others feel important involves three aspects: a look, a word, and a touch.

A Look: When you meet someone, stop what you are doing, look them in the eye and give them your undivided attention. For the few moments that you are greeting them, they should feel like they are the most important person on earth to you.

And don't forget to smile! Actions speak louder than words. A sincere smile says, "I like you and am glad to see you." If you want people to be happy to see you, you need to show them that you are happy to see them.

Being reminded to smile seems childish. But I need the reminder. I am a thinker by nature. (Now that I am a professor, my sons delight in calling me an absent-minded professor.) I reminded myself to smile until it became a habit. Funny thing . . . the more I smile, the more people smile back at me.

A Word: When you meet someone, say something when you look them in the eyes. It may be as simple as the word "Hello." Your tone should indicate you are genuinely glad to see them.

If you have not met the person before, ask for his or her name and introduce yourself. When acquaintances share their names, make sure you get the proper pronunciation and repeat it back to them. If you can use their name a few times in the conversation without it seeming awkward or contrived, you'll find it is a power bridge builder. Using his or her name in your first conversation while looking the person in the eyes is also a great way to commit their face and name to memory.

A Touch: Each time an appropriate touch is made, relational walls come down. If you are meeting someone for the first time, a handshake is often most appropriate. Or, you can touch their elbow or shoulder. If you already know each other or have not seen each other in a while, a hug may be the right touch. Some cultures are very "touchy" while others are not, so consider the background of each person you meet and respond appropriately.

The power of a name

> *The man who enters by the gate is the shepherd of his sheep... the sheep listen to his voice. He calls his own sheep by name and leads them out... his sheep follow him because they know his voice. But they will never follow a stranger; in fact, they will run away from him because they do not recognize a stranger's voice.* (John 10:2-6)

Jesus taught the value of shepherds knowing their sheep "by name." Effective leaders know their sheep by name too. Never forget the sweetest sound in any language is the sound of one's own name.

The summer after Cathy and I were married, we led a group of 35 college students who worked in a church in Manhattan. I was there the year before, so the pastor already knew me. But he did not know Cathy and he never made the effort to learn her name.

Just to be ornery, Cathy did not go out of her way to remind him of her name. All summer long—and for the years following—he tried to speak with her without using her name. He referred to her when speaking to others as "Dave's wife." Needless to say, Cathy did not have as much loyalty or respect for him as a leader. He failed to make the effort to learn her name, and thereby failed to be an effective leader in her life.

Just three new families a week

When planting a church years ago, we had an average of three new families visit our Sunday services each week. When I made the effort, it was not difficult to learn the names of the visitors each week. I would call them on Monday evening and tell them I would be looking for them the next Sunday.

Every week I reviewed their names and prayed for them, then called them to tell them I would be looking for them to come back for a second visit. Many did. When they arrived, I made a point of calling them by name. This always made a positive impression. Our members would bring guests up to me and tell them, "If you come back, Pastor Dave will remember your name."

To make the job easier, after the second week they visited out church I snapped a Polaroid picture of each family and wrote their names on the back. By learning the names of three new families a week, and by reviewing the previous ones, I was able to remember the names of hundreds of families.

I could stand at the front door on Sunday mornings and greet everyone coming in by name. By doing this, I earned the right to speak into their lives later during the teaching time. It also had a positive effect when I was around town during the week. When I called out to people who had visited our church a few times by name to greet them, many returned to our church services that next week.

Don't say, "I can't remember names." Most people can't remember names because they do not take the time and effort to *secure* the person's name, *review* the person's name, and *use* the person's name.

Every time you meet someone you will make a deposit or a withdrawal. Learn to make deposits by using their names to make people feel important.

Honor others.

"Be kindly affectionate to one another with brotherly love, in honor giving preference to one another" (Romans 12:10).

I have two colleagues. Both have PhDs and are respected professors. One is very popular and loved by his students. The other? He is not as well-loved. The first leads a thriving ministry. The second professor pastors a church, but it's dying.

What is the difference? Although what I am about to share is not the entire reason, it does adequately summarize it.

Whenever I see the first one, who is loved by others, he always smiles and looks me in the eyes, always says my name, and works hard to find something affirming to say about me. I walk away from him feeling better about myself.

The other always makes a dig, a cut, or a cute comment. He is belittling, condescending, and patronizing. He rarely gives a compliment. When I walk away, I feel like I have been depreciated.

Nothing builds a relationship more than the atmosphere of esteem and honor. Nothing erodes it more than a climate of disrespect. When a leader breathes an atmosphere of respect and regard, followers respond. People respect people who respect them.

Below is a chart that shows the difference between actions that honor others and actions that take advantage of them. Which column best reflects your actions?

Actions that Honor Others	Actions that Dishonor Others
Words of appreciation and affirmation	Disapproval, criticism, or cut downs
Giving credit	Taking Credit
Taking initiative to clear up misunderstandings	Refusing to act first to resolve misunderstandings
Only criticizing in private	Criticizing in front of others
Asking others for their opinions	Failing to seek the opinions of others
Updating people on their status, progress, or anything else that may affect them	Keeping people in the dark by withholding information
Impartiality	Favoritism
Active listening (giving a person one's full attention)	Disinterest
Noticing when a person needs encouragement and offering it	Failing to notice the condition of others

Humble yourself in order to elevate others.
"All of you, clothe yourselves with humility toward one another" (1 Peter 5:5).

A full translation of this verse would read, "Clothe yourself in a servant's apron of humility." This means we are to adopt or "wear" the attitude of a servant when we are around others. Servants understand that everything they do is all about their masters, not about them.

Effective leaders also understand that it is not all about them. They do not expect to be served by their followers. Instead, effective leaders look for ways to focus on and serve those they lead.

I enjoy being around people who are interested in me. When they ask about my family, my interests, and my point of view versus talking about themselves, I feel valued. One of the most effective ways to build a relationship with others is to humble yourself and focus on their interests and opinions. Think and speak in terms of their point of view. Remain interested in them instead of trying to get them interested in you. If you practice this kind of others-focused interaction, people will be drawn to you and your small group.

Actively serve others.
"You, my brothers, were called to be free. But do not use your freedom to indulge the sinful nature; rather, serve one another in love" (Galatians 5:13).

Jesus, of course, is the model servant. His act of leaving Heaven, coming to earth, being born as a baby, and dying for us was a stunning example of servant leadership (see Philippians 2:5-9). He told His disciples that His purpose in coming was not to serve, but to serve and give His life for others (Mark 10:45). Beyond that, even at the most personally stressful season of his life, hours prior to his arrest and crucifixion, he took a servant's towel and washed their feet (John 13:1-6). Jesus was a leader who was followed because he was a leader who served His followers.

Servant leadership is an attitude that translates into action. It is a mind set that results in ministry. Servant leadership is humbling yourself to meet the needs of others. It is washing their feet (John 13:14). It is trying to help make them successful.

Give others the freedom to be themselves.
"Accept one another" (Romans 15:7). (Also see Romans 14:13.)

Over the years I have enjoyed a close interaction with two pastors who lead a couple of the largest churches in America. Both are brilliant, gifted, and hard-working leaders.

Yet, one made me feel uncomfortable. I came away from our meetings feeling as if I did not measure up. The second leader gave me greater acceptance and I liked him much better. I wanted to help him fulfill his vision, and would gladly labor to aid his success.

When people sense a spirit of criticism or self-righteousness in a leader, they either shrink back, close down, or grow defensive. A spirit of criticism will snuff the life out of a follower. On the other hand, unconditional acceptance becomes fertile soil to foster deep relationships and grow new leaders.

Everyone responds favorably when they sense they are accepted unconditionally. Additionally, people will follow you as their leader when they can be themselves and still feel loved and accepted.

Communicate with others.
"Instruct one another" (Romans 15:14).

Relationships live or die based on communication. Effective leaders are effective communicators.

When I was starting out in ministry, I had the same job, but two different bosses during my first two years. The first year was absolutely miserable. My first boss never took the time to communicate with me. When I asked him for direction or feedback he was either too disinterested or too busy to give it. I felt insecure and unsure of my performance and quality of work. I was hesitant to try new things, kept my opinions to myself, and worked hard to stay out of his way. Because of his lack of communication, I was a hinderance, not an asset.

My second year on the job was blissful. I had a new boss! He made it a point to communicate quickly, clearly, and regularly. It did not take much of his time, but it made all the difference in the world in my level of performance. I went out of my way to please him and gladly helped him in several areas outside my job description. I loved working for him and we remain close friends.

What was the difference in the two? My second boss employed excellent people skills and understood the value of communication.

Don't try to win every argument.
"Submit to one another" (Eph. 5:21).

One summer I worked on a janitorial crew that stripped and waxed the floors of a school building without air conditioning. It was an unusually hot and humid summer, making our work a very hot and difficult task.

All of the guys on our crew were studying to be pastors. During our breaks—as is common with young pastors-to-be—we discussed theological views. This made waxing floors in a hot building far more interesting.

There was one fellow, Stanley, who always had to be right. In his mind, he was never wrong about anything. He would argue his points relentlessly, winning every argument he could. Since Stanley was the only guy on the crew who was actually pastoring a church, he felt he was the ultimate authority on *everything* (how to strip and wax floors, choosing the best sandwich meat, and so on). He loved confrontation and pushing people's buttons.

Whoever was assigned to be Stanley's work partner had the worst day ever. Hearing his ranting throughout the entire work day was misery. His unsubmissive attitude made him very difficult to be around and no one wanted to work with him.

I guess our summer work crew weren't the only ones who felt this way. A few years later, his arrogant attitude caught up with him. His church asked him to resign and then his wife filed for divorce. Ouch!

Most arguments are not worth winning. In the big picture of life, it won't make any difference. The arrogant leader that must win every argument and always be right will soon have no one to lead. Community grows when people are willing to submit to one another and "agree to disagree" on preferential issues.

Resolve conflicts.
"Live in genuine harmony with each other" (Romans 12:16).

Conflict is inevitable. To deny or avoid conflict will only create superficial relationships and erode intimacy. Conflict is also necessary. God allows it in every relationship and small group. Resolving conflict builds unity and community.

When conflict comes—and it will come—the wise leader will initiate steps to resolve it. Here are a few basics to move through conflict.

First, pray for discernment. Ask yourself, "Is there really a conflict or am I just being overly sensitive?" Many choose to take offense when the person in question simply chose the wrong words or could have phrased what they said in a better way. You must always look at the *intent* of the other person before assuming he or she meant harm with what was done or said.

Second, take ownership of your share of the problem. Many conflicts are two sided and the action of the other person is actually a *reaction* to something you may have done or said. Always approach a conflict with this in mind, asking the person if their attitude or actions are a result of something you have done or said to offend them.

Third, determine the best time to talk privately with the person, which is probably as soon as possible. Or, you may need to wait until you are calm and have collected your thoughts. But don't wait too long. In either case, begin your conversation by explaining this might not be a *comfortable* conversation, but it is an *important* one.

If you discover you are the primary source of offense, I recommend that you employ these "twelve simple words for resolving conflict." (I am not sure where I first heard them, but I have used them frequently with great success.) They are:

"I was wrong"

"I am sorry"

"Please forgive me"

"I love you"

If the other person is the primary source of offense, you must begin by affirming the value of your relationship by communicating this as the reason you want to resolve this conflict. Ensure they know you care about your relationship enough to talk about the situation openly. Then share what you have observed in terms of what was seen, heard, and felt. Don't make accusations. Ask the person how he or she perceived the situation. Then try to gain a mutual understanding. If the person uses some of the twelve simple words to resolve the conflict, accept the apology and move on.

Encourage others.

"Encourage one another" (1 Th. 5:11; Heb 3:13; 10:25).

People gravitate toward those who see the best in them. Encouragement is oxygen to the soul! Encouragement also creates relational collateral. The word *encouragement* speaks of "coming alongside of another to give them courage." Living for God in a godless world can be a fearful challenge. Everyone needs a leader behind them saying, "I believe in you. You can do it."

I challenge you to make a habit of encouraging others every time you visit with them. Point out their progress. Remind them of their past successes. Take notice of their present investments. Express belief in them for the future. Spur them to do the right things in their life and ministry.

If you develop the heart of an encourager, you will find that people are excited to be around you and will readily follow you.

Remain sensitive to others.

"Be kind and compassionate to one another, forgiving each other, just as in Christ God forgave you" (Eph 4:32).

Excellent leaders build a family atmosphere. This is expressed first by loving all the people all the time regardless of what they are going through. Even if a person is having a bad day, and in spite of the fact he or she is enduring a challenging set of circumstances, the person feels loved. It means being kind to them when they are unlovable and taking note of the fact they are hurting, remaining sensitive to their pain.

Unity is deepened as you go through tough times together. It further deepens as you continue to bear a burden with someone, and when necessary, offer forgiveness. Let me remind you, forgiveness is not a feeling. It is a choice. Forgiveness is not forgetting what someone has done—which may be impossible— but choosing to treat the person as though the offense had never been committed.

Never gossip or slander others.
"...do not slander one another" (James 4:11).

As a leader, you have privileged information about people that others might not know. This information may be inaccurate, one sided, or negative. Or, the information is very personal and intimate.

You must learn to practice verbal discipline, giving careful consideration to how you refer to or comment about others. You must not share information that you are not sure is true (which is gossip). You must not share someone else's personal or intimate information (also gossip). You must also withhold false information about another (slander) or a truth that will put them in a bad light (also slander).

Refuse to gossip about or slander someone when they are they are present, but especially when they are absent. Why? First, it is a sin. Second, it teaches your followers to do the same to each other and to you. Third, it offends the person being slandered or gossiped about, especially if they are not present and hear about what you said from someone else.

Everyone has a horror story of a relationship that was short-circuited by slander or gossip. Slander and gossip will always come back to hurt you and tarnish your character.

Love others.
"A new command I give you: Love one another. As I have loved you, so you must love one another. By this all men will know that you are my disciples, if you love one another" (John 13:34-35).

Jesus said the essence of being people-skilled comes down to one thing: love. The encouragement of this command is that He tells us to love one another in the same way He loves us. This is challenging. He loves us with an amazing unconditional, undeniable, unrelenting, and unstoppable love. His love for us is sacrificial and selfless. It always seeks to do what is best for us. It is also the key to effectively leading people.

His command to love one another as He has loved us is also encouraging. We don't naturally possess that type of love. The Holy Spirit produces the fruit of love for others as we yield control of our lives to Him. As God loves people *through* us, we will be able to apply all the other "one another" commands with ease. We will intentionally use greetings to make others feel important. We will honor them. We will gladly humble ourselves to elevate others and serve them.

As a Spirit-filled lover, you will become accepting, giving people the freedom to be themselves. You will naturally make the effort to communicate and resolve conflict, even when it is uncomfortable or difficult. You will be encouraging and sensitive of others, never gossiping about or slandering them.

Some people skills come naturally while others require practice and hard work to integrate into your leadership style. Use the worksheet on the following page to learn more and grow in this area.

As you develop the people skills described in this chapter, you'll have one more leadership tool to help you become—or remain—successful as a small group leader.

The Small Group Leader PEOPLE SKILLS Worksheet

1. List the first and last names of everyone in your group.

_____

_____

_____

_____

_____

_____

_____

2. Read through these ways we are to love another with each member in mind before you move on to the next exercise. Take your time and reflect on each one as it pertains to the individual members of your group.

Use greetings to make others feel important.

Honor others.

Humble yourself to elevate others.

Actively serve others.

Give people the freedom to be themselves.

Communicate.

Don't win every argument.

Resolve conflict.

Encourage others.

Be sensitive.

Never gossip or slander.

Love others.

3. How would the members in your group respond to your people skills in each of these areas if they were grading you in each area?

Use greetings to make others feel important .❑ Poor ❑ Average ❑ Great

Honor others . . . .❑ Poor ❑ Average ❑ Great

Humble yourself to elevate others . . . .❑ Poor ❑ Average ❑ Great

Actively serve others . . . .❑ Poor ❑ Average ❑ Great

Give people the freedom to be themselves . . .❑ Poor ❑ Average ❑ Great

Communicate . . . .❑ Poor ❑ Average ❑ Great

Not try to win every argument . . . .❑ Poor ❑ Average ❑ Great

Resolve conflict . . . .❑ Poor ❑ Average ❑ Great

Encourage others . . . .❑ Poor ❑ Average ❑ Great

Be sensitive . . . .❑ Poor ❑ Average ❑ Great

Never gossip or slander . . . .❑ Poor ❑ Average ❑ Great

Love others . . . .❑ Poor ❑ Average ❑ Great

4. Now underline the skills in which you want or need to improve.

5. Write down the specific things you know you must apply in order to increase the relational deposits you have with each small group member:

_____

_____

_____

_____

_____

_____

_____

Chapter Eight
PERSUASION

Every so often when I read my Bible, something leaps off the page and captures my full attention. Even though the pages of my Bible are printed in black and white, a phrase will burst off the page as though it is in neon lights and twice as large as the rest of the words.

A few years ago, I was reading the Gospel of John and these verses jumped straight off the page at me:

> *And as He walked by the Sea of Galilee, He saw Simon and Andrew his brother casting a net into the sea; for they were fishermen. Then Jesus said to them, "Follow Me, and I will make you become fishers of men." They immediately left their nets and followed Him.* (Mark 1:16-18)

Woah! They *immediately* left their nets and followed Him. They did not flinch or hesitate.

Jesus was an amazingly effective leader. How do I know? When He called, people followed. Being a leader is not having a title: it is having followers. It is like the Chinese proverb: He who thinks he is leading and has no one following is only taking a walk. Leaders must not only be high quality persons who know where they are going, they must be able to take others with them.

As I continued reading Mark's gospel about Jesus' leadership, it happened to me again.

> *When He had gone a little farther from there, He saw James the son of Zebedee, and John His brother, who also were in the boat mending their nets. And immediately He called them, and they left their father Zebedee in the boat with the hired servants, and went after Him.*
> (Mark 1:19-20)

Wow! These men were willing to walk off their day jobs and even away from their families to follow Jesus. As we know from studying the history of the day, this was not the first time they had met. They tracked Jesus' ministry from a distance for a year and liked what they saw. When He invited them to become His apprentices, they jumped at the opportunity.

Let me ask you three tough questions. Do you have followers? Are people lining up to become your apprentices? Are you willing to learn to lead in such a way that people cannot help but follow you?

As I study the life of Jesus as it relates to leadership, I see eight principles He practiced that made him a leader his disciples would die for. In order to help me remember them, I put them in the form of an acrostic that spells the word "persuade."

HOW DID JESUS PERSUADE OTHERS TO FOLLOW HIM?

P: Positive Expectations

Jesus took an average group of men and motivated eleven out of the twelve to become world changers. How did he do it? He used the power of positive expectations.

A study of first century Hebrew culture shows that rabbis selected the brightest young men for rabbinical training at an early age. By the age of fourteen or fifteen, most of the young men were sent home to learn the family business because they failed their examinations. Only a small and privileged group of brilliant students who passed the rigorous tests could then apply to a well-known rabbi to become one of his disciples.[1]

When Jesus came to Peter, Andrew, James, and John and said, "Follow me and I will make you fishers of men" He showed great confidence in them when others had shunned them. Can you imagine what it must have been like to have a rabbi say, "Come, follow me"? No wonder they dropped everything to follow Him! He was giving them a second chance they never imagined they would receive. He believed in them. He had positive expectations for their future. He saw them as leaders and they fulfilled His expectations.

Dr. Robert Rosenthal of Harvard University discovered that expectations become self-fulfilling. He performed an interesting study with students and lab rats.

He informed his students that they would be training rats to validate breeding techniques. He assigned the first group of students to train rats that were bred for *superior* intelligence. The second group of students were assigned to train rats bred for *average* intelligence. The third group of students were assigned rats bred for decidely *low* intelligence.

The students were instructed to train the rats to run through a maze as quickly as possible and note their behavior and speed. After six weeks, the students reported that the smart rats performed exceptionally, the average rats were simply average, and the slow rats did poorly running through the maze.

As you might have guessed, there were no "genius" rats bred for superior intelligence. They were all average rats out of the same litter! The difference in performance was purely derived from the expectations of their human handlers.

In 1964, Rosenthal performed his experiment again, but this time he selected public school teachers and students. The teachers were given the names of children in their school supposedly identified by a new test as being on the verge of blooming intellectually. The children, however, had been chosen at random.

At the end of the school year, the selected children showed greater gains in intellectual abilities compared with the other children. Moreover, teachers perceived the children in the ''bloomer'' group as more appealing, adjusted, and affectionate than the others.

Over the next few years, Dr. Rosenthal reviewed 345 studies showing the power of the "teacher-expectancy effect." Again and again, additional research has revealed that students perform twice as well as other students when they are expected to do so.

Effective small group leaders harness the power of positive expectations to motivate others. They believe their followers can rise up and make a difference *and* they communicate that belief.

What would happen if you began to see the potential in yourself that Jesus sees? What would happen if you began to see the potential in your small group members that Jesus sees? What if you went out of your way to communicate this to them?

Make Application

How will you show Positive Expectations to raise the bar for your group members in the next 30 days? Write it here:

E: Exposure

Jesus motivated His disciples not only by giving them purpose, but also by exposing them to several important issues.

Allow them to get to know you (Mark 3:13-14, Matt. 17:1-13).

If you are becoming a person who possesses a strong prayer life, personal integrity, a deep passion, and clear priorities, then potential followers will want to know you better. Jesus gave the disciples short glimpses into Himself, slowly exposing more and more of Himself to them. When He called them to follow Him and become fishers of men, they were eager to act. They wanted to spend more time with Him and see what made Him tick.

I tend to be more of a project person than a people person. I can default into becoming overly guarded. Several years ago I read a book that helped me become a better leader. The author, Alan Loy McGinnis, shared two sentences I really needed to read:

> People with deep and lasting friendships may be introverts, extroverts, young, old, dull, intelligent, homely, good looking; but the one characteristic they always have in common is openness. They have a certain transparency allowing people to see what is in their hearts.[2]

Notice the words "openness" and "transparency." We will never compel people to follow us into spiritual leadership if we do not learn to become open and transparent. We need to move beyond merely sharing facts and opinions and learn to share our true feelings, our struggles, and our delights.

Expose them to the need (John 4:35, Matt. 9:36-37).

People become hungry to follow when they see the need. Jesus was intentional about exposing His followers to the need. Jesus intentionally went out of His way to minister to the Samaritan woman. He capitalized on it as an opportunity to expose His followers to the harvest and the reality that they could play a role in reaping it. This exposure to the need became motivation for them to serve:

> Do you not say, "There are still four months and then comes the harvest?" Behold, I say to you, lift up your eyes and look at the fields, for they are already white for harvest! ... I sent you

to reap that for which you have not labored; others have labored, and you have entered into their labors. (John 4:35-38)

Expose them to themselves (Luke 9:1-6, Mark 1:17).

Jesus motivated His followers by exposing them to Himself, to the need at hand, and to themselves. He put them in situations where they could experience their potential through letting them taste success:

> *Then He called His twelve disciples together and gave them power and authority over all demons, and to cure diseases. He sent them to preach the kingdom of God and to heal the sick. … So they departed and went through the towns, preaching the gospel and healing everywhere.* (Luke 9:1-6)

Jesus also placed them in settings where they encountered their shortcomings by allowing them to fail without him:

> *And when they had come to the multitude, a man came to Him, kneeling down to Him and saying, "Lord, have mercy on my son, for he is an epileptic and suffers severely; for he often falls into the fire and often into the water. So I brought him to Your disciples, but they could not cure him." … Then the disciples came to Jesus privately and said, "Why could we not cast it out?" So Jesus said to them, "Because of your unbelief; for assuredly, I say to you, if you have faith as a mustard seed, you will say to this mountain, 'Move from here to there,' and it will move; and nothing will be impossible for you. However, this kind does not go out except by prayer and fasting."* (Matthew 17:14-21)

Make Application

How will you use the principle of Exposure to provide more effective leadership for your group members in the next 30 days? Write it here:

R: Recognition

In 1936, an unknown YMCA instructor named Dale taught a course on human relations that was so popular he compiled it in written form. When he published his little book, *How To Win Friends and Influence People,* it remained on the best-seller list for 10 years, a record that still stands today. It's sold over 15 million copies globally and sells at a rate of 200,000 a year.

In this book, Carnegie shares one truth he calls "the big secret in dealing with people." It's nothing new or unusual. In fact, Jesus used it 2,000 years ago. What was Carnegie's big secret? "Be hearty in your approbation and lavish in your praise."[3] (The word *approbation* is the act of formally approving, commending or praising.) He discovered that people respond positively when they receive honest and sincere appreciation.

Abraham Lincoln was a very persuasive leader. Leading America through one of the toughest times in its history, he motivated people to make great sacrifices to finish a very bloody war and unify the nation. He keenly observed, "Everybody likes a compliment."

Carnagie and Lincoln weren't the only famous men in history to address recognition. Mark Twain once said, "I can live for two months on a good compliment."

Good people have labored unnoticed for long periods of time. Eventually, they grew weary and productivity dropped off. When those same workers received recognition for their hard work, they labored far longer and at a higher level of productivity.

During our annual school banquet, my high school wrestling coach gave out several trophies recognizing outstanding achievements. At my first banquet, I watched upperclassmen win those awards. I determined that by the time I graduated I would win as many as possible. Over the next few years, I put in a ton of extra work and discipline motivated by the goal of receiving that recognition at the banquet.

Believers should be motivated to labor diligently to receive awards of eternal value at the "heavenly awards banquet." But wise leaders do not overlook the reality that even good Christians are spurred on to greater efforts when their earthly spiritual leaders recognize their efforts.

I have yet to meet the person who did not respond favorably to positive recognition. Wise leaders take notice when others are working hard and recognize it.

Make Application

How will you use the principle of Recognition to provide more effective leadership for your group members in the next 30 days? Write it here:

S: Significance

On average, I speak in 35 different churches each year. At a recent event, the lead pastor complained that none of the members desired to become small group leaders. He also whined about not having anyone willing to do some necessary Sunday morning duties such as teaching preschoolers.

After he made his Sunday morning announcements, I quickly understood why no one was excited about signing up to serve. With a sigh he said, "Once again, we need someone to help in the preschool on Sunday mornings." Everyone in the congregation dropped their heads and became very occupied reading their bulletins. He then went on to say, "I know that it is a tough assignment . . . I certainly wouldn't want to do it. But if someone would just suck it up and volunteer, we would all be appreciative."

With that kind of presentation it was no surprise that no one signed up!

Three weeks later, I was in another church. When it came time for the announcements, a brightly dressed lady in her fifties practically ran up to the mic. "I am so very honored to stand before you today!" she gushed. "I get to tell you about an incredible opportunity. In a few minutes I will give you a chance to register your interest, but I need to warn you ahead of time, only a few can be accepted at this time."

She smiled widely and said, "A few of you will have the opportunity to invest two hours each week to change the course of history." At this point I was highly curious about this marvelous opportunity.

And with that, she made her pitch. "The chosen few will get to plant the seed of God's Word deep into the hearts of future world changers."

Like the rest of the congregation, I was on the edge of my seat and she had my full attention. She continued with, "Our church is growing so rapidly that we need to add another preschool class. Of course, we won't be able to take all of you, but if you want to help us change the world, one preschooler at a time, please sign the card in your bulletin and bring it to me after the service."

Her presentation was so motivating I started looking through my bulletin for the card. My wife grabbed my arm and whispered, "We live in another state, Dave. I don't think you can commute eight hours to work in the preschool department of this church."

Jesus motivated His disciples to go out and change the world by pointing out the supreme significance of their task. He described their task as being:

- Global in scope — *"all nations"* (Mt. 28:19-20, Luke 24:47); *"the ends of the earth"* (Acts 1:8).
- Regal in nature — *"the kingdom of God"* (Luke 9:1-2, 60).
- Eternal in time — *"that food which endures unto everlasting life"* (John 6:27).
- Impossible in challenge — *"without me you can do nothing"* (John 15:5).
- Essential in importance — *"As my Father has sent me, I am sending you"* (John 20:21).
- Greater in quality — *"greater works than these shall you do"* (John 14:12).

Someone observed that the deepest urge in human nature is the desire to be important. You must learn to recruit to a vision and use the power of pointing out significance. I believe that fulfilling the Great Commission by cooperating with Jesus in building His church is the most significant task anyone can do. Do you?

The moment you believe that your ministry as a leader is not supremely significant, you are in trouble. If your small group is not a God-anointed agency of life change, you had better change your group or have the integrity to close it down. If it is what it should be, never be embarrassed to trumpet that reality to the ends of the earth!

Make Application

How will you use the principle of Significance to provide more effective leadership for your group members in the next 30 days? Write it below:

U: Unselfishness

Motivational leaders are sacrificial leaders. Jesus motivated His disciples by His evident example of unselfishness. Even though He was and is God, He chose to see things from the perspective of His followers. Effective persuaders connect with their followers by seeing things from their perspective. Thomas Aquinas once said that when you want to convert someone to your view, you go over to where he is standing, take him by the hand (mentally speaking) and guide him. You don't stand across the room and shout at him, you don't call him a dummy, and you don't order him to come over to where you are. You start where he is and work from that position. That's the only way to get him to budge.

Jesus is the King of Kings and Lord of Lords. His worth is beyond measure, and His glory is beyond description. Yet, He motivated his followers to serve others because He served them. He washed their feet. The disciples of Jesus endured extreme sacrifice and suffering for the cause. They faced persecution, beatings, prison and even martyrdom because they had seen Him endure the same.

Wise leaders understand the power of unselfish leadership. One of America's most successful football coaches, Paul "Bear" Bryant had a simple philosophy of coaching and motivation. He said:

> I'm just a plow hand from Arkansas, but I have learned how to hold a team together - how to lift some men up, how to calm down others, until finally they've got one heartbeat together, a team. There's just three things I'd ever say: If anything goes bad, I did it. If anything goes semi-good, we did it. And if anything goes real well, then you did it. That's all it takes to get people to win football games for you.

Make Application

How will you use the principle of Unselfishness to provide more effective leadership for your group members in the next 30 days? Write it below:

A: Affection

We have all heard the saying, "People do not care how much you know until they know how much you care." It is true. Followers are motivated by evident love and affection.

Jesus was an affectionate leader. He expressed his love for His followers by…
• Serving them (John 13:1,4-5)
• Selecting them (John 15:13, Mark 3:13)
• Stating their position as friends (John 15:13-15)
• Sticking with them after they failed (John 21:3-17)
• Showing them physical affection (John 13:23)

I did not grow up in an openly affectionate home. I had to learn the power of affection on my own. I have discovered that sincere and appropriate affection is very powerful.

When our church was young and filled with young believers, we asked the Lord for a spiritually mature couple to help us. God graciously provided when Dan and Patricia moved into town from out of state. They were everything on my prayer list: doctrinally sound, spiritually mature, willing to work with young people, and experienced in leadership. But they were a few things I had not prayed for that showed up unexpectedly. Dan was very crusty. His grandparents raised him because his parents were alcoholics. He was always "constructively critiquing" us as leaders and we could never do anything right.

We decided to use the power tool of affection on Dan. Our youth pastor, who gives a great hug, made it a point to hug Dan whenever he saw him. I invited Dan to be a member of my men's leadership group that met weekly. Because we lived in the same neighborhood, Dan drove me to the home where the group met. When he dropped me off the first night, I turned to him and said, "See you Sunday, Dan. Don't forget that I love you, buddy."

The "I love you, buddy" must have taken him by surprise. He just looked at me and mumbled, "Uh . . . ur . . . see you Sunday."

The next week when he dropped me off in front of my home, I hit him on the arm and said, "See you Sunday, Dan. I love you, buddy."

He kind of dropped his head and mumbled, "Well . . . uh . . . my wife likes your wife a lot."

The third week that he gave me a ride, I gave him the "I love you, buddy" goodbye. He looked down and said, "Well, my wife and I like your kids a lot." He was thawing!

The fourth week, I said, "See you Sunday, Dan. Never forget that I love you, buddy."

Dan looked down and let out a deep sigh, saying. "Pastor . . . " he paused, sighed again, then with a pained look on his face said, "I love you too."

I looked over and saw a tear roll down his cheek.

"Thanks, Dan" I said. "You don't know how happy we are to have you and Patricia at our church." Then he just put his head down and gulped.

The affection was getting through. After that night, Dan was a different man. He laughed more. His comments shifted from critical to helpful and encouraging.

A few years later, Dan was transferred out of state with his job. Not long after, I was at a pastors' conference and I happened to see his new pastor and I asked how Dan was doing.

"Great! Dan and his wife are great people" he said. "They really miss your church," he continued. "You must have one of the greatest churches in the world," he said with a grin.

"What do you mean?" I asked.

"All they do is talk about what wonderful leaders you and that youth pastor are." He said, "I don't know what you did, but they really love you."

Make Application

How will you use the principle of Affection to provide more effective leadership for your group members in the next 30 days? Write it below:

D: Demonstration

Jesus motivated His disciples by clarifying three essential truths. He told them:

- *What* He expected: make disciples (Matthew 28:19-20).
- *Why* it was important: people are lost (Matthew 9:36-38).
- *How* they could do it (Matthew 9:27-35, 10:1-15).

I coached little league sports for many years. Without reservation, I can say that the primary tools to motivate children to participate and play hard is taking the time to show them what, why, and how. Good coaching is not about yelling. It's about showing, just like Jesus did with his disciples.

One year, I inherited a baseball team of eight-year old boys. They had a 2 win-12 loss record the year before, finishing thirteenth out of fourteen teams. Their teamwork was sloppy, their esteem was shot, and they possessed no hope of achievement in the new season.

When I called each team member's home before the start of the season, the parents shared disappointments concerning the previous summer. They also revealed that their children said they would not play any more sports if they did not have a good baseball season. The pressure was on!

Our first practice was a nightmare. Most of the boys showed up late. Watching them warm up was painful because they couldn't field, hit, run, or throw. Neither could most of their parents! Everyone was frustrated and unmotivated.

I called them together and asked every dad present to become an assistant coach. When they agreed, I used the power of demonstration to turn around this losing team and show them how to be winners.

We started with the four basic skills of baseball: running, fielding, throwing, and hitting. We broke down each skill and explained what, why, and how. My sons demonstrated how to do it. Then the boys—with their dads—practiced the skills, carefully reviewing the "what, why and how." By the end of that first practice, they could run to the right bases in the right direction and some were even fielding the ball. Best of all, they were motivated to come back to the next practice.

The second, third, and fourth practices reinforced what they learned at that first practice. We carefully demonstrated the four basic skills of baseball again and again: running, fielding, throwing, and hitting. We broke down each skill and explained "what, why, and how." Then, the boys practiced the skills with their dads. Slowly, they got the hang of fielding, throwing, and hitting.

By the time we played our first game we were running, fielding and throwing respectively and somehow we won the game. I suggested that we have an extra voluntary practice each week, curious to see how many would show up. I was shocked when all the boys came out (as well as most of their fathers).

Some of the dads told me they had always wanted to play baseball when they were kids, but no one ever showed them how. They were learning along with their sons and loving it.

The result? Our team ended up being the surprise of the season. We finished second out of fourteen teams!

I am convinced that people are naturally motivated until they are de-motivated. Often, all an unmotivated person lacks is someone to show them how to do something well.

Think about it. There are people in your group who will become amazing leaders if you will take the time to teach them how to serve the other members in some way and lead various parts of the meeting.

Make Application

How will you use the principle of Demonstration to provide more effective leadership for your group members in the next 30 days? Write it below:

E: Encouragement

One of my favorite stories in the book of John is found in the last chapter. Because of his threefold denial of Christ, Peter was extremely discouraged. He felt so insufficient to do ministry that he went back to the comfort of fishing. Jesus found him and the others on a boat. They were failing without Him, but after heeding His advice, they caught a miraculous number of fish. Then Jesus uncovered His skillful touch of a master motivator.

> *So when they had eaten breakfast, Jesus said to Simon Peter, "Simon, son of Jonah, do you love Me more than these?" He said to Him, "Yes, Lord; You know that I love You." He said to him, "Feed My lambs." He said to him again a second time, "Simon, son of Jonah, do you love Me?" He said to Him, "Yes, Lord; You know that I love You." He said to him, "Tend My sheep." He said to him the third time, "Simon, son of Jonah, do you love Me?" Peter was grieved because He said to him the third time, "Do you love Me?" And he said to Him, "Lord, You know all things; You know that I love You." Jesus said to him, "Feed My sheep."* (John 21:15-17)

There is so much I could write about this passage. But let me draw your attention to one major truth: Jesus verbally encouraged Peter.

Three times Peter denied Jesus, and three times Jesus commissioned him to feed the Master's flock.

Peter left this encounter with needed direction and zeal for the task at hand. Later, we read that Peter preached the gospel before a huge crowd, where 3,000 people responded to the invitation to accept Jesus as their Messiah and Savior.

Elsewhere in John's Gospel, Jesus motivated His disciples by giving them appropriate doses of encouragement. Notice the many different ways he encouraged them . . . He encouraged them with his example (John 13:15), His love (13:35; 15:9,12), His return (14:3), the promise of sending another encourager (14:16), the promise of a resident power source (14:20), His friendship (15:15), and by showing confidence in them (15:16).

One of the devil's favorite devices is discouragement. At various times everyone becomes discouraged. We all need someone who is in our corner, on our side saying, "Keep going. Don't quit. I am with you. You can do it!"

Make Application

How will you use the principle of Encouragement to provide more effective leadership for your group members in the next 30 days? Write it below:

The Effective Small Groups Leaders PERSUASION Worksheet

Read through the eight keys to motivating followers and circle the ones you are doing well:

Positive Expectations

Exposure

Recognition

Significance

Unselfishness

Affection

Demonstration

Encouragement

Now underline the ones you in which you most need to improve.

Reading back through the applications you wrote at the end of each principle, write down *three big ideas* you can apply in order to be a more persuasive leader.

1. _____

_____

_____

2._____

_____

_____

3. _____

_____

_____

Chapter Nine

PEOPLE DEVELOPMENT

Several years ago I was obsessed with reading the gospels to discover how Jesus lived and did ministry. I did not unearth anything new or groundbreaking, but it did impact my life. Jesus' ministry can be distilled into three primary areas. He loved all, taught many, and equipped a few.

Jesus loved all

Jesus loved people. He fed the hungry, healed the sick, and taught the ignorant. Out of a deep love for people, He left heaven to come to earth and die for our sins.

Jesus really loved people. He preached the good news to all with whom He came in contact. In chapter seven of this book, I wrote about people skills with the "one another" commands of the New Testament. Jesus was the master model of great people skills as He fleshed out what it means to love one another.

Jesus taught many

Jesus did not merely share information. He brought true transformation into the lives of His followers. Today He clearly serves as a template for each of the characteristics of a powerful persuader. He gave His followers strong doses of positive expectation, exposure, recognition, significance, unselfishness, affection, demonstration, and encouragement.

Jesus equipped a few

Jesus' most significant ministry was not feeding the multitudes. It was not even teaching the crowds. It was training the few.

Jesus trained twelve Jewish men so He could reach an entire world of Greeks, Romans, Asians, Germans, Indians, Arabs, Latinos, Russians, and Americans. The training of the twelve was the primary global ministry strategy of Jesus Christ. He knew He would have to leave. He also knew one of His disciples would fail, but He never wavered from His plan. His plan hinged on eleven trained leaders. His plan to reach the whole world—generation after generation—was simple. Train a few to reach the many. That was His plan and it should also be yours.

It is not enough to lead through prayer, personal integrity, passion, purpose, priorities, or planning. It is not sufficient to love people so they like you enough to follow you. Nor is it enough to motivate others to action. Real leaders also develop others.

Jesus equipped Peter, James, and John. Barnabas mentored Paul and later, Mark. Paul poured his life into Silas, Timothy, and Titus. Who are you training?

Effective small group leaders help move others from where they are to where they could be. They are "people enlargers." They disciple and develop, equip and empower, mentor and mobilize.

WHY YOU SHOULD DEVELOP OTHERS

There are many reasons why every effective leader must invest a portion of their lives into mentoring rising leaders. Four stand among many.

1. Developing others keeps you sharp and growing.

My old nature is lazy. Without external prompts I coast along. Soon enough, I find myself satisfied with the lowest level of personal growth.

This changes when I mentor others. If I am pushing them to memorize Bible verses, I must memorize as well. If I challenge them to read a helpful book, I must be reading too. When I encourage them to share their faith, I must share my faith.

Mentoring others keeps me growing. Currently, a large part of my ministry is with college and seminary students. Investing in them keeps me young and enthusiastic. I plan to mentor others throughout my life to stay sharp and keep growing. How about you?

2. Developing a few can impact many.

I started a church with eleven adults who met in my basement. Within a few years, those eleven adults led eight multiplying small groups. In time, those eight groups multiplied to 125 small groups for adults and teens. Our church ministered to nearly two thousand people a week and planted several new churches.

A small group leader can positively impact approximately ten families at time. You have a choice. You can nurture ten families and your impact will stop at those ten families (which isn't a bad thing, really). Or, you can intentionally develop a few leaders with the same amount of time and energy. By equipping a few leaders, you can impact hundreds of others. By training *multiplying* small leaders, you can influence thousands of people!

Yes, multiplying leaders is a seemingly small, slow, and unappreciated process at first. But what is exciting to 'ordinary' people like you and me is that by using a process of multiplication, we can have a big impact. Believe it or not, multiplying leaders reaches the most people in the least amount of time.

3. Developing others leaves a legacy.

Everyone desires a legacy. We all want to be remembered fondly after we are gone. Multiplying leaders is a great way to have an impact after we are off the scene.

Jesus left His disciples as His legacy when He ascended into heaven. Yet the ministry of Jesus has grown and multiplied many, many times over because His disciples were multiplying leaders. He showed us that if we spiritually multiply ourselves today, we will start a dynamic process that could reach beyond our generation and into the next century.

4. The fulfillment of the Great Commission hinges on people development

Of the five times Jesus gave the Great Commission (Matthew 28:19-20; Mark 16:15, Luke 24:45-47; John 20:21; Acts 1:8), the richest is the Matthew 28 passage:

> *Go therefore and make disciples of all the nations, baptizing them in the name of the Father and of the Son and of the Holy Spirit, teaching them to observe all things that I have commanded you; and lo, I am with you always, even to the end of the age. Amen.*

A deeper look at this passage reveals that the primary phrase in this commission is *make disciples.* Everything else tells how to do it (*go, baptize, teach*). The overlooked aspect of this passage is that we have not made a disciple until they are doing everything Jesus commanded His disciples to do. Therefore, the process is not done when we have led a person to trust Jesus as their Savior. That is only the beginning. We also must develop them to the point where they can reproduce other spiritual reproducers. So, the fulfillment of the Great Commission hinges on us spiritually developing disciples.

The slow process of equipping multiplying leaders is the fastest way to fulfill the Great Commission. The world is growing rapidly by biological multiplication while the church is growing slowly through spiritual addition. In order to catch up and keep pace with the multiplying population of the world, we must multiply spiritual multipliers.

IF YOU DON'T DEVELOP OTHERS...

There are many good reasons to invest your time in developing others. Conversely, there are many liabilities that come from failing to develop others and multiply your ministry. When we fail to train future leaders we inadvertently force passionate and gifted individuals to remain on the bench. Potential leaders will exit your group or even your church because they are looking for a place where they can make a contribution. You and your group will never reach its potential if you have not developed others to reach their personal potential.

WHAT IS PEOPLE DEVELOPMENT?

Several years I ago, I crystallized what I understood about multiplying new small leaders. It became the book, *Turning Members into Leaders*. In chapter seven, I defined the leadership tool of people development as, "the process of cooperating with God by using every available resource to help another person become a multiplying small group leader."[1] Let's break down this definition to better understand and apply it.

First, developing others is a process, not an event. This means it takes time and involves multiple steps. People development requires taking someone from one level to another at their own pace.

Second, it is cooperating with God. God is in the process of developing leaders. He works in ways that are deeper, more powerful, and more effective than we could ever do on our own. He will use circumstances and events. He will use all elements of His body. Therefore, the job of the multiplying leader is simply to cooperate with what God is already doing. (This is why I stated prayer as the primary component of the multiplying leader's toolkit.)

Third, development requires using every available resource. Some of the resources available to the multiplying leader include classes, on-the-job training, books, tapes, workbooks, and personal mentoring.

Fourth, it is helping another person become a multiplying small group leader. How do you know if you have done the job? The answer is obvious. The other person is effectively leading a group that is multiplying leaders.

Why leaders neglect to develop others

There are many excuses for neglecting to develop others, but none of the following should exclude you from raising up others to lead!

Too insecure — Some leaders fail to develop others because they are too insecure in themselves. They wrongly think they have nothing to offer an apprentice. Or, they feel threatened if the apprentice turns out to be more successful or a better leader.

In order to effectively develop others, you must find your security in Christ and get to the business of multiplying your ministry by training others.

Too egotistic — You have heard the old saying, "Some people are so egotistic that they either have to be the bride at the wedding or the corpse at the funeral." They wrongly think that leading a group is all about them and others exist to serve them.

Never forget that it is not all about you and your ministry. The moment you think it is, your effectiveness as a people developer is over. It is about God's kingdom. It is about reaching a needy world and helping others succeed.

Failure to discover the potential in others — God has gifted everyone with the raw materials to become a difference maker. Your job as a leader is to diligently, prayerfully, and painstakingly help others see this. Once they do, you must aggressively help them nurture it with encouragement and opportunity.

"I never had a mentor." — Most have never had a person come alongside to pour into their lives and raised them up to leadership. So they think they have no experience out of which to mentor others. Being unsure of what to do, they do nothing. Have you ever thought this?

The truth is you have probably had *several* models God used along the way to help you get to where you are as a leader. Recognize who has invested in you and consider what each person taught you. Take the best practices learned from each person along the way and apply these to raising up new leaders from your group.

"I don't know how."— This excuse may have worked in the past, but it simply doesn't hold water any longer. In the rest of this chapter I will share with you how to mentor others. (If this is not enough, I suggest that you read my book, *Turning Members into Leaders,* as it is an entire book devoted to the subject of mentoring multiplying apprentices.)

FOUR STEPS FOR DEVELOPING OTHERS

There are four primary steps in developing others. They work in both the micro and the macro level of leadership development. What I mean by this is that each works in training another to lead a ministry time in a meeting (micro), or in developing another to lead a group (macro).

Model — In the macro level, the most powerful way you will influence others is with your example. Your life shows them not only what a leader does, but also who a leader is. You must model the right beliefs, values, attitudes, as well as activities and demonstrate the tools of effective leadership. Show them you have a strong prayer life, godly personal integrity, the right priorities, compelling purpose, wise planning, hard work, and good people skills.

Good leadership models understand the value of allowing their apprentices to watch them in action. They never do ministry alone. For this reason, make it a habit to take a potential leader with you when you minister to others. Let them see you doing it and show them how it is done.

On the micro level, effective leaders show their apprentices how to do various activities of facilitating a small group meeting. Simply put, the multiplying leader leads the activity and the potential leader watches. This might cover any or all of the activities needed to lead an effective group. This includes: making phone calls to group members, planning and executing a small group social event, visiting a member in the hospital, leading the group ice breaker or prayer time, or preparing the agenda.

These ministry activities may come easily for you, but they are intimidating to a potential leader. Demystify the activities for the potential leader by modeling them.

Mentor — Mentoring on the macro level is taking your apprentice under your wing and being interested in every aspect of his or her life. It is being highly concerned about the person first, then the training and skill development they need to be a great leader. Mentoring involves coaching the person through various life situations and ministry opportunities.

On the micro level, mentoring occurs when the multiplying leader shows the potential leader how to do an activity well, inviting the potential leader to watch and learn. Afterward, the multiplying leader gives the potential leader encouragement to do the same activity soon and learn from their experience.

For example, I often take apprentices with me to visit a group member in the hospital or at home on bed rest. I ask them to watch me as I do most of the talking. After we leave, I ask them what they saw me do and why they think I did it that way.

Micro modeling could involve practice sessions or role-playing. I might ask an apprentice to develop discussion and ministry questions for a small group meeting and share them with me as if we were in an actual meeting.

Motivate — I have learned that one of my primary tasks as a people-developer is to encourage potential leaders. On the macro level this means I not only see their potential, but I point it out to them, affirm it, and applaud it. I am the person in their life whom they know believes in them.

On the micro level, the multiplying leader motivates disciples by stepping back and trusting the potential leader to lead. I accompany them as they visit one of our group members in the hospital. I let them do most of the talking and I am there as a safety net. Afterward, I share several things they did well, and point out only one thing they could improve upon.

Motivating may also involve trusting them to lead an entire small group meeting while you participate as a member. Then, motivating them more involves trusting them to lead in your absence. This could be as simple as being out of the room to being out of town.

I am currently training a church planter. He is especially motivated when I turn over teaching opportunities to him and tell him I trust him to handle it.

Multiply — Multiplication is your goal. You must see your apprentice serving as an independent and highly effective leader.

On the micro level, you have multiplied yourself when the potential leader consistently leads without your direct supervision. You may remain involved as a coach, but for all practical purposes, the person is leading on their own. This will begin with making phone calls and leading the elements of the group meeting. It eventually leads to the potential leader taking over your group, launching their own group, and developing an apprentice of their own.

Putting the four steps together

There are several key elements to being an effective multiplier. Some involve activities that must be performed outside the group: praying for group members, inviting new people, contacting absentees, preparing for the group meeting, and planning social and outreach activities. Other key elements involve leading the actual small group: the Welcome (icebreaker); the Worship time, the Word (Bible application and ministry time), and the Witness (praying over the unchurched friends who will be invited to the group).

In order to develop someone to take your place to lead a group session, you must train the person to do every aspect effectively. What follows is an example of how the four-step development process might occur on the micro level:

Jason invited Adam to be his apprentice last month. Each week, they meet the night before the group meets to pray and prepare. This is how Jason developed Adam to lead the icebreaker:

Model it. *I do it – you watch.* Week one: Jason prepares of the four elements (Welcome, Worship, Word, and Witness). Adam watches and asks questions. Jason explains what, why, and how he creates these elements so Adam can learn Jason's developmental process.

Mentor it. *You do it – I help.* Week two: Jason helps Adam prepare the icebreaker. He practices it in front of Jason. Jason offers encouraging and helpful comments. Then, Adam leads the icebreaker in the group the next night. Jason gives him more encouragement and helpful feedback when they get together in their weekly meeting.

Motivate it. *You do it - I watch.* Week three: Adam creates and shares the icebreaker by himself. Jason tells the group how proud he is of Adam and what a great job he's doing as the group's apprentice.

Multiply it. *You do it.* Week four, Adam handles the icebreaker on his own from now on, showing other members how to do it as well.

Since Adam has mastered the Welcome portion of the meeting (sharing the icebreaker), Jason leads Adam through the same four steps to develop Adam to confidently lead the Worship time.

By learning one new element a month, Adam will be ready to lead an entire group session by the end of five months. During this time, Jason will use the four step process to show Adam how to perform outside-the-meeting ministry activities.

After five or six months, Adam may be ready to lead his own group. However, if I were the coach over this group, I would strongly suggest that Jason take several additional months to ensure that Adam is living the eight primary outside-the-group habits of an effective small group leader: Dream, Pray, Invite, Contact, Prepare, Grow, Fellowship/Party, and Mentor (for more information on these eight habits I suggest that you read my book, *Eight Habits of an Effective Small Group Leader*).

ADDITIONAL ADVICE

Make people development a high and continual priority.

It is easy to let this element of leadership slide, but you must not do so. Your ministry legacy and greatest joy will be the people you took the time to develop and release.

Focus on the few.

Remember, Jesus loved all, taught many, but only equipped a few. Remember the 80/20 rule of prioritizing? We should spend 80% of our time with the top 20% of our people who have the greatest potential to multiply.

Build the relationship

There are three times we need to focus on building a relationship with future leaders. First, build the relationship before you begin leadership development. People "buy into" you before they "buy into" your leadership. Second, build the relationship as you develop them. Ministry runs on the train track of growing relationships. Don't become so focused on the process that you forget the person! Third, continue to build the relationship after you have multiplied. People I have mentored often become my closest friends. By developing a relationship with those you mentor, they will know you consider them to be friends, not projects.

Don't give up

You will certainly pour your life into some people only to see them wash out. Even Jesus had a washout, so keep at it! You will break through with more people than you think, so don't give up if the first person you train doesn't become a leader. Think of it this way: if you only train one other truly effective multiplying leader in the next five years, you will have struck a serious blow, advancing the kingdom of God!

The Effective Small Group Leader's PEOPLE DEVELOPMENT Worksheet

Consider the person you are currently training to be a small group leader. How well are you doing in the four basic areas of development?

Modeling . . . .❑ Poor ❑ Average ❑ Great
Demonstrating effective small group leadership for a member of your group, who clearly understands he or she is to observe and learn as part of a leadership development process.

I must clearly demonstrate the following leadership tasks or roles for my potential leader:

1. _____

2. _____

3. _____

4. _____

5. _____

Mentoring . . . .❑ Poor ❑ Average ❑ Great
Remaining interested in every aspect of a potential leader's life and encouraging the person to lead out in group activities and meeting roles with you.

I must do the following to invest more time into my apprentice in the areas of friendship and ministering/leading together:

1. _____

2. _____

3. _____

4. _____

5. _____

Motivating . . . .❏ Poor ❏ Average ❏ Great
Purposely giving an increasing level of responsibility and credit to your apprentice as you step back to show them you trust them.

I must give away the following leadership responsibilities to my apprentice to motivate them and give them a heightened sense of ownership:

1. _____

2. _____

3. _____

4. _____

5. _____

Multiplying . . . .❏ Poor ❏ Average ❏ Great
My apprentice has the heart of a small group leader and is leading the group. I am helping him or her develop a future leader successfully and I clearly see my leadership legacy.

I must incorporate the following values into my leadership development plan to ensure each apprentice I train is a multiplying leader:

1. _____

2. _____

3. _____

4. _____

5. _____

Complete as much as you are able on this worksheet and review it with your small group coach or pastor quarterly to view progress.

Chapter Ten
PARTNERSHIP

A Tale of Two Groups

A married couple has led a small group for two years, which meets in their apartment. Every week, the wife rushes home from work to clean the apartment and make snacks for the guests. The husband dashes home from work too, changes clothes, grabs a sandwich, and rushes back out to pick up a family and their four kids (who don't have an operating car). When the husband arrives, he immediately starts the meeting by sharing the icebreaker. Then the wife leads the worship. After a few songs, the husband leads the Bible discussion while the wife takes the ten unruly kids to another room for a Bible lesson and crafts. Then, the wife switches roles with her husband as she leads the ladies in a prayer time while he watches the kids.

Many of the members of their group are new believers with struggling marriages and a lot of baggage. So, they need an extended sharing time. When the meeting is finally over at 10:30 p.m., the wife picks up around the house, which has been trashed by the ten children. Of course, the husband isn't there to help because he's returning the family without a car back to their home!

This couple does not want to be a bother to anyone, so they have not asked a group member to serve as an apprentice. They also told their pastor not to worry about them and they could get by without a coach.

Throughout the life of their group, this couple has done all the inviting, contacting, and inviting for the group. They have been so busy that they rarely have the time or energy for prayer. As you can easily surmise, they are worn out and discouraged. On more than one occasion, they have discussed resigning from group leadership and leaving the church.

Josh and Ashley lead a very different kind of small group. Josh and Ashley's group meets in a different home each month. Their group has eight children, and different group members turns working with the kids. Different group members also share the responsibility of picking up and taking home Maria and her kids each week, since her husband works most evenings and has the family car.

Josh and Ashley were wise enough to develop apprentice leaders for their group to prevent burn out. Ben and Megan share the responsibilities for praying for the group members daily, contacting them weekly, and inviting new people to the group. They also help plan and play a role in the social events the group enjoys. With their current level of participation, they will be ready to launch a new group soon.

Josh and Ashley anticipate growth and have prepared for it. They have helped Ben and Megan find a couple in the group to serve as their apprentices when they start their group. Plus, Josh and Ashley are investing additional time into a married couple who joined the group a few months back so they will have apprentices in their next group.

Josh and Ashley have found that everything works better if they take time to pray for their group. They pray together about their group a few minutes each day before work. On Sunday mornings, they invest a half hour before leaving for the church service to pray for each member by name.

Josh and Ashley also utilize the support their church offers them. Karen is their coach and visits with them or visits their group regularly. Josh and Ashley love leading a group and find that leadership actually gives them energy. They don't know what the future holds, but they hope they can remain in small group leadership for many years to come.

What is the difference between the first couple and Josh and Ashley? The answer is simple: teamwork! Josh and Ashley employ the leadership tool of partnership.

Four types of partnerships

There are four primary avenues where you, as a wise and effective small group leader, must fully employ the power of partnership to enjoy your ministry.

You with God

God is the most obvious — but often most neglected — partner you have when you minister to others. Fruitful ministry is simply cooperating with what He is already working to accomplish. As Paul reminded the Corinthians, you do your part, but it is God who gives the increase. This is why prayer is the first tool of the highly effective small group leader.

You with those above you

Every effective small group leader needs a coach. Leaders need a fresh, unemotionally-involved set of eyes to see problems accurately. They need an encouraging word when times are difficult, an experienced voice when tough situations arise, and inspiration to remained focused on the task at hand.

You with those beside you

Small group leadership is too vital and challenging to do alone. Develop a co-leader to share the load and you will find that leadership is fun.

You with other group members

Never think that by doing all the work, you are serving others. This is a faulty notion. Your role, in part, is to get others involved. People grow by doing ministry versus receiving ministry. The more people in your group who have taken ownership, the greater the liklihood that it will succeed.

Involve as many group members as possible to pray for the group and contact other group members between meetings. Lead your group members to invite new people. Encourage them to plan and execute group fellowship or outreach events. The more they do, the better!

NEVER UNDERESTIMATE THE POWER OF PARTNERSHIP

Teamwork is one of the greatest forces on earth. Unfortunately it is also the most neglected. Solomon was the wisest man who ever lived. He was also a strong believer in the power of partnership. He wrote:

> *It's better to have a partner than go it alone. Share the work, share the wealth. And if one falls down, the other helps, But if there's no one to help, tough! Two in a bed warm each other. Alone, you shiver all night. By yourself you're unprotected. With a friend you can face the worst. Can you round up a third? A three-stranded rope isn't easily snapped.*
> (Ecclesiastes 4:9-12, *The Message*)

Solomon's wise words still thunder out truth today. Never underestimate the power of partnership! According to Solomon the power of partnership produces greater accomplishment (Ecc. 4:9), increased encouragement (Ecc. 4:10), enhanced spiritual temperature (Ecc. 4:11), and stronger resilience (Ecc. 4:12). Effective leaders never underestimate the power of partnership.

Get more done for God (Ecc. 4:9)

Solomon observed that when we "share the work, we create more wealth." In other words, when we work in partnership, we get more accomplished. Teamwork divides the task and doubles the achievement.

Our church modeled teamwork in everything we established. The church was launched by a team of eleven adults. Every small group and ministry was a team effort. The deacons worked together as a team. Why? Because we believe teamwork is Biblical. We operated under the simple T.E.A.M. principle:

TOGETHER EVERYONE ACCOMPLISHES MORE

Because eleven adults were working together, we were able to multiply our ministry until it grew to nearly 2,000 members. One small group multiplied into 12, plus dozens of others were launched in five new churches we started.

The essence of successful partnership is synergy . . . the theory that the outcome of the whole is greater than the sum of the parts. For example, one man owned two oxen. Both oxen could pull seven hundred pounds a piece. But yoked together, they could pull 1600 pounds.

Speaking on the power of synergy, Tom Cheney writes:

> A student of mine works for United Parcel Service (UPS). His job is loading the brown trucks – a grueling task that involves much lifting. A prerequisite to employment is the ability to lift 70 pounds by one's self, or 150 pounds with a partner. Now in grade school I learned that 70 and 70 totaled 140, not 150. Can it be that UPS understands the scriptural truth behind Ecc.. 4:9 better than many church leaders?

"I have fallen ... and I can't get up!" (Ecc. 4:10)

"And if one falls down, the other helps, But if there's no one to help, tough!" (*The Message*).

"I have fallen and I can't get up!" was a catch phrase of the early 1990s pop culture. It came from a television commercial for a medical alarm company. In the commercial, an elderly lady has fallen in the bathroom and has no one to help her up. She presses a button on the handy pendant worn around her neck and is immediately put into contact with an emergency dispatcher.

Life is tough. Everyone goes through rough and troublesome times. We all get knocked down from time to time. The power of partnership is that we have someone to help us get up when we are knocked down.

Hot for God (Ecc. 4:11)

Who hasn't been hot for God, only to see the flame die quickly? Partnership produces an enhanced spiritual temperature. The fire of God in the life of others is a tool God uses to rekindle our flames and keeps us burning brightly for Him.

Practically unstoppable (Ecc.. 4:12)

"By yourself you're unprotected. With a friend you can face the worst. Can you round up a third? A three-stranded rope isn't easily snapped" (Ecc. 4:12, *The Message*).

When you step up to lead, you move to the front lines of ministry and to the forefront of spiritual warfare. The enemy places a bigger target on your back and the spiritual attack intensifies. This would be a very dangerous place to be if it weren't for the power of a team. If you have two or three close partners in ministry, you can face almost anything the enemy can throw at you! There is an old Kenyan Proverb that states the following:

"STICKS IN A BUNDLE ARE UNBREAKABLE"

Individual sticks can be snapped with ease. By banding many together, they become far more difficult to break. One of the enemy's chief strategies against leaders is to try to get them alone and torment them. We need each other. Together we are practically unbreakable.

We need each other! (1 Corinthians 12:12-27)

> *But now indeed there are many members, yet one body. And the eye cannot say to the hand, "I have no need of you"; nor again the head to the feet, "I have no need of you." No, much*

> *rather, those members of the body which seem to be weaker*
> *are necessary... And if one member suffers, all the members*
> *suffer with it; or if one member is honored, all the members*
> *rejoice with it.*   (1 Corinthians 12:20-26)

The apostle Paul's favorite metaphor for the church was the body of Christ. He marveled how under Jesus (our head), we work in a unity of diversity and mutual dependency just like a healthy human body. We are many members (1 Cor. 12:12, 14), yet, we are but one body (1 Cor. 12:12-13). Every member is distinct (1 Cor. 12:14-20), yet interdependent on the others (1 Cor. 12:20-27).

No body part survives, let alone thrives, in isolation. Just as God created each of us with a God-shaped void in our hearts, He also created us with a human-shaped one. We need other people. Wise leaders recognize their need for one another and build their small groups into a fully functioning team and a powerful partnership.

ROADBLOCKS TO PARTNERSHIP

Leaders fail to utilize the power of partnership for many reasons. Some of the more common roadblocks to teamwork are described below.

Ego
There is no "I" in "TEAMWORK." Partnership occurs when ministry is no longer about "me" but all about "we."

Some leaders suffer the hazards ego-driven isolation, missing out on the power of partnership. Face the facts . . . you need God and, you need others. No one can reach their spiritual potential by doing ministry alone. Our sovereign God divinely placed the people in your small group for a reason. He has given you everything and everyone you need to fully serve Him.

Insecurity and jealousy
Some leaders fail to realize the power of partnership because they are not secure enough to handle it when others can do what they do. Don't let the bottleneck of your impact be you. Let me encourage you to find your security in Christ and turn others loose to serve.

Naiveté

Unfortunately, some leaders have yet to recognize the potential power of partnerships. Hopefully by reading this chapter you have been convinced of your desperate need to work with others.

A reserved or "loner" temperament

I am an introverted loner by nature, content to quietly do my own thing. But I cannot deny what the Bible teaches about the power of partnership. I recognize that it is not good that I should minister alone, and I have seen firsthand the benefits of teamwork. I have also felt the pain of trying to go it alone. I have seen the light and been converted! I will never do ministry in isolation again. I know that I need God and others. So do you.

Impatience

Leaders, by nature, are confident people. Some are an active, impatient, and restless bunch, confident they can do ministry easily and quickly. Assuming leadership is easy, they haphazardly delegate tasks and watch the person fail miserably. So, the impatient leader takes the responsibility back and refuses to teach others.

This is a big mistake. If this describes you, you must let others try and fail. You must patiently continue to teach, train, and involve others until they are proficient. If you don't, your ministry will be limited to you alone.

ESSENTIALS FOR BUILDING TEAMWORK

A common and compelling goal

When my youngest son was five, he wanted to play soccer. His team was crushed in their first game, which was painful to watch.

The coach was a well-meaning young man who insisted on doing everything himself, which was clearly not working. He knew a lot about soccer, but very little about children.

At the time, soccer fields were in high demand, and five-year-olds were the lowest priority for the league. So, my son's team practiced in a barren field without soccer goals. The coach attempted to teach the kids complicated drills they did not understand. After just a few weeks, practices degenerated into little kids kicking each other or chasing butterflies. They were bored and complained of being too hot, too tired, needing a drink, or having to go to the bathroom. The parents were bored too . . . spending most of their time milling about, complaining about the coach.

One afternoon during practice, the coach received an important phone call and had to leave for a few minutes. He looked in my direction and asked me to take over practice until he returned.

The first thing I did was set up two goals using water bottles. Then I called the children over and explained to them that the goal of soccer was to kick the ball into a goal. Then I got all the parents who were milling around to help me divide the kids into two teams and practice kicking the ball into the goals. Every kid had the opportunity to kick the ball through the goal. Then we practiced passing the ball to a teammate so they could kick the ball into the goal.

The coach returned to find his little soccer players smiling and laughing. They were fully engaged and very excited. No one whined for a drink, or needed a rest, or required a potty break. They were working together. They parents were happy and relieved to see their kids enjoying practice.

His jaw dropped and he asked, "What happened?"

"Teams need goals," I said. "Otherwise they cease to be teams. Everything you were trying to show them did not make sense to them without having the goals."

Small groups and churches become teams only when they work together to achieve a common goal. Some small groups are dead and lifeless because the leader is the only one working to achieve the goal. Often, these leaders grow weary as their groups drift in the sea of purposelessness.

Goal-oriented groups are vital and thriving. People are excited to be a part of it and morale is high because everyone is pulling together in unity of purpose. Personal agendas are set aside to achieve the goal of worshipping the Lord, reaching the lost, and serving one another.

Wise leaders find their group's passion and help the members define the group's purpose. They keep this purpose in the minds of their members by sharing it often, which reinforces the need for teamwork.

Shared ownership of the goal

Often teams do not gel because everyone is on a different page. While we are all different, we must all pull together around one purpose. Teams function effectively to the extent that all the members buy into the same goal.

Effective small group leaders constantly speak in terms of "we." They talk about the purpose and show how every person can be involved in carrying it out that purpose. They include every willing person in the group building process. And, they bring everyone along who wants to come.

Do you possess characteristics of an excellent team player?

Through research and reflection on my own experience, I created a list of the characteristics of excellent team players. These characteristics are qualities all Spirit-filled believers should manifest. Moreover, the small group leader must model these characteristics to lead the way for his or her group.

An excellent team player . . .
1. Consistently places the needs of the team ahead of self.
2. Is willing to admit his or her mistakes.
3. Is willing to forgive others and move on.
4. Avoids the trap of petty jealousy.
5. Consistently shares the credit with others when things go well.
6. Maintains a positive attitude.
7. Refuses to hold a sour, critical spirit.
8. Is free of the "disease of me."
9. Is willing to be held accountable.
10. Is willing and able to pay the price.
11. Shares the same core values as his or her pastoral leaders.
12. Remains a consistent and willing communicator with other group members and church leadership.

This chapter's worksheet will help you discover just how much of a team player you are today and where you can improve. I challenge you to distribute the first page to two or three members of your group and ask them for honest feedback. The second page provides a place for you to rate yourself on the characteristics found above and write out a plan of action for change. These worksheets may be tough to work through, but you'll become a much better leader if you complete them.

Partnership: Last but not least

Partnership is the final power tool in your toolkit, and it is one of the most important tools you can use as a small group leader. It reduces leader burn-out and mobilizes others to lead and minister alongside you. Abandon any thoughts of leading your small group alone! When used with the other tools found in this book, partnership will transform you and your group members from a collection of individuals to a kingdom-building team.

The Effective Small Group Leaders PARTNERSHIP Worksheet

*Make copies of this page and ask your spouse, apprentice, and/or one or two close friends
from your small group to complete it with you and give you honest feedback.
Take it yourself as well and see how you view yourself compared to those you respect.*

1. Do you see me as a team player?
❑ No. ❑ Some of the time. ❑ Most of the time. ❑ All of the time.

2. Do I place the needs of the group members ahead of my own?
❑ No. ❑ Some of the time. ❑ Most of the time. ❑ All of the time.

3. Do I readily admit my mistakes?
❑ No. ❑ Some of the time. ❑ Most of the time. ❑ All of the time.

4. Am I a person who is willing to forgive and move on?
❑ No. ❑ Some of the time. ❑ Most of the time. ❑ All of the time.

5. Have you seen me become jealous when others received credit for our group's success or someone leads out in our group?
❑ No. ❑ Once or twice. ❑ It happens frequently.

6. Do I share the credit for our success with others in the group?
❑ No. ❑ Some of the time. ❑ Most of the time. ❑ All of the time.

7. Do I maintain a positive, upbeat attitude?
❑ No. ❑ Some of the time. ❑ Most of the time. ❑ All of the time.

8. Am I a good communicator as the leader of our small group?
❑ No. ❑ Some of the time. ❑ Most of the time. ❑ All of the time.

9. Do you view me as a person who holds a sour, critical spirit?
❑ No. ❑ On great occasion. ❑ Yes.

10. Is there anything else about my leadership of our group that you would like to discuss with me?

Personal Questions

Out of the twelve areas of being a team player found on page 135, choose the two areas in which you feel require improvement. Now, write down what you must do differently to improve in both areas:

1. _____

_____

_____

2. _____

_____

_____

To whom will you be accountable? What must you share with them to increase your level of partnership as a leader? Write the person' name below and describe what you must share when you meet:

_____

_____

_____

_____

If you realize you've been doing ministry alone, or you're burned out as a small group leader, ask God to carry the burden and show you who is ready to help you lead your group. Write out a prayer here:

_____

_____

_____

_____

CONCLUSION

Congratulations! Between the gifts and blessings God has lavished upon you in Christ and the practical skills taught in this and other books, you have what it takes to make a difference in the lives of others. As a person of prayer, integrity, passion, priorities, purpose, and planning you can effectively lead yourself deeper into maturity. As a person of persuasion, people skills, and people development, you can successfully lead others! God can and *will* use you as a leader.

But reading this book must not be the end of your leadership journey. It is just the beginning of an exciting adventure of high impact living. To state it another way, remember that it is one thing to have a garage full of great power tools. It is another to actually use them with proficiency.

Use the Tools

My father was the least mechanical person I have known. He taught me many valuable things in life, but never how to fix or maintain anything. His goal was to earn enough money to pay other people to do it for him, or he would just let the item deteriorate. So, in my twenty-five years as a home-owner, I have paid careful attention to my neighbors, trying to learn how to maintain a home and care for my power tools. Through observation, I discovered there are differing approaches to the care and use of home and lawn care equipment.

Take Jim for example. He had the newest and nicest equipment of anyone in the neighborhood. But many of his tools never made it out of the garage. It was as though he did not want to get them dirty. For example, he had a new snow-blower, but hated to take it out in the cold. All of his tools were neatly displayed, hanging from pegs on the back wall of his garage. Yet, his fancy equipment never helped anyone else, and rarely helped him.

Then there was Brian, who also had wonderful power tools. He was a bit fanatical with what he owned. He cleaned and polished his edger, lawn mower and weed whacker after every use. He washed his cars by hand every Saturday too. While he used his equipment for his own property, he was completely repulsed at the thought of helping a neighbor or ever sharing his tools for any reason. He had the best snow-blower in the neighborhood, but he only used it for the front of his own house.

Tony, a third neighbor, had a few older, well-worn tools that he used regularly. Tony was also generous, allowing me to use them occasionally.

The best was an older neighbor. Mr. Riggs not only used his tools regularly and wisely, but he helped me select my tools. Then he went the extra mile and showed me how to use and maintain them.

When it comes to the equipment in your leadership toolkit, my desire is that you will use them to bless yourself and your family and that you will use them to help others. Beyond that, it would be wonderful if you invested part of your life in showing others how to acquire and put into practice the leadership gear God has made available to all leaders. In other words, use your tools and show others how to use theirs.

Get your money's worth

You have invested your time to read this book. In order to maximize your investment, I suggest that you go back through the book and complete the worksheet at the end of each chapter if you have not done so already. It will not take long, but it will pay huge dividends.

I also suggest that you develop an accountable relationship with someone who will help you to follow through with what you know God is pressing you to do. Give your pastor, coach, co-leader, apprentice, spouse, or friend permission to ask you how you are doing in your weakest areas. Information only leads to transformation when it is coupled with application.

END NOTES

Introduction

1 Quoted by Elmer Towns, *The Eight Laws of Leadership*, (Lynchburg: Church Growth Institute, 1992), p. 10.

2 Major Branches of Religions Ranked by Number of Adherents: http://www.adherents.com/adh_branches.html#Christianity.

3 Walt Henrichsen, *Disciples are Made Not Born*, (Wheaton: Victor Books, 1979), p. 143.

Chapter One

1 J.O. Sanders, *Spiritual Leadership*, (Chicago: Moody, 1974), pp. 82-84.

2 For a full and practical explanation of the link between prayer and spiritual leadership, see my book, *Praying With Giants*, (Chattanooga: AMG, 2008).

3 Hudson Taylor, as quoted in J.O. Sanders, p. 82.

4 Andrew Murray, *The Prayer Life*, (Springdale: Whitaker House, 1981), p. 8.

5 Joel Comiskey, *Home Cell Group Explosion*, (Houston: TOUCH Publications, 1998), p. 34.

6 John Wesley and John Calvin, quoted by Peter Wagner in *Prayer Shield*, (Ventura: Regal books, 1992), p. 29.

7 Billy Graham quoted by Cort Flint, editor, *The Quotable Billy Graham*, (Anderson: Dort House, 1966), p. 154.

8 Charles Spurgeon, *Pray Without Ceasing*, Metropolitan Tabernacle Pulpit, A sermon delivered on Sunday, March 10th, 1872, http://www.spurgeon.org/sermons/1039.htm, (accessed June 30, 2008).

9 Martin Luther quoted by E.M. Bounds, *Power Through Prayer*, (Grand Rapids: Zondervan, 1962), p. 37. Italics added.

10 Mike Fearon, *Martin Luther*, (Minneapolis: Bethany House, 1986), pp. 156-157.

11 Paul Y. Cho, *Prayer: Key to Revival*, (Waco: Word Books, 1984), p. 18.

12 Eastman, *No Easy Road*, (Grand Rapids: Baker Book House, 1971), p. 58.

13 Eastman, p. 57.

14 Wagner, p. 26.

15 Wesley Duewel, *Mighty Prevailing Prayer*, (Grand Rapids: Zondervan, 1990), p. 22.

16 Bounds, p. 27.

17 S. D. Gordon, *Quiet Talks on Prayer*, (Grand Rapids: Baker Book House, reprinted 1980), p. 44.

18 Story told by H. Begbie in *The Life of General William Booth* as recorded at http://www.jesus-is-savior.com/Great%20Men%20of%20God/general_william_booth.htm

19 D.L. Moody, *Prevailing Prayer*, (Chicago: Moody Press, 1987), pp. 100-101.

20 Basil Miller and George Muller, *Man of Faith and Miracles*, (Minneapolis: Bethany House 1943), p. 146.

21 Miller, p. 146.

22 Adapted from Greg Frizzell, *How to Develop a Powerful Prayer Life*, (Memphis: Master Design Ministries, 1999), p. 83.

Chapter 2

1 Dave Ramsey, *The Truth About Bankruptcy*, http://www.daveramsey.com/the_truth_about/bankruptcy_3018.html.cfm (accessed June 30, 2008).

[2] Stan Toler, *Four Keys to Good Character*, (Stan Toler's Leadership Letter, Vol. 5, No. 3).

[3] Pat Means, *Men's Secret Wars*, (Ventura: Revell, 1996), pp. 132-133, 255.

[4] 1992 survey of *Christianity Today* readers (one-third pastors, two-thirds laymen; 80% active in church leadership; 810 respondents), printed by "CT Marriage and Divorce Survey Report" CT, Inc., Research Department, July 1992.

[5] Dr. Archibald D. Hart, *1994: The Hart Report* (confidential survey of 600 men), printed by *The Sexual Man*, (Waco: Word Books, 1994), page 95.

Chapter 3

[1] The well-known acrostic S.M.A.R.T. was introduced in the book, *The Pocket Guide to Leading a Small Group*, by Dave Earley and Rod Dempsey, (Houston: TOUCH Publications, 2007), p. 192.

[2] Ann Rusnak, *The Secret to Making Goals Happen*, http://www.mrmomentum.com/articles/yourgoals.html, (accessed April 4, 2008).

Chapter 4

[1] George Barna, *Leaders on Leadership*, (Ventura: Regal Books, 1997), p. 54.

Chapter 6

[1] Alan Lakein, *How to Get Control of Your Time and Your Life*, (New York: New American Library, 1973), p. 25.

[2] Leroy Eims, *Be the Leader You Were Meant to Be*, (Colorado Springs: Cook Communications, 1996), p. 55.

[3] Joel Comiskey, *Leadership Explosion*, (Houston: TOUCH Publications, 2000), p. 34.

[4] Joel Comiskey, *Cornerstone Cell Group Leaders Training Conference*, Staunton VA, November 9, 2007.

Chapter 8

[1] Rob Bell, *Velvet Elvis*, (Grand Rapids: Zondervan, 2006), chap. 5.

[2] Alan Loy McGinnis, *The Friendship Factor*, (Minneapolis: Augsburg Press, 1979), p. 17.

[3] Dale Carnegie, *How To Win Friends and Influence People*, (New York: Pocket Books, 1964), p. 40.

Chapter 9

[1] Dave Earley, *Turning Members into Leaders*, (Houston: TOUCH Publications, 2003).

CPSIA information can be obtained
at www.ICGtesting.com
Printed in the USA
BVHW042151310122
627716BV00013B/615